THE
MACHINE · KNITTER'S
HANDBOOK

Welcome to the craft of Machine Knitting!

REASONS for wanting to own a knitting machine are many and varied, but for most of us once the desire has arisen it will not go away until it has been satisfied and the box containing all those mysterious-looking bits and pieces is sitting on the kitchen table.

If knitting has always meant wool and needles up to now, a machine is a very new and strange object, however keen you are to learn to use it. No one who has been machine knitting for a short time can fail to sympathise with a new knitter unpacking the machine for the first time. 'What's this?' 'Where does this go?' And later on: 'Why did it do that?' – Plus a few other rather less genteel remarks. These early attempts to get to grips with the machine are often accompanied by feelings of dismay at having spent a considerable amount of money, and the growing fear that you will never be able to use the thing capably.

However every experienced machine knitter will admit to having gone through this stage, so take heart. Press on and you'll be surprised how, with a little patience, your enthusiasm will carry you forward and you will quickly gain mastery of the machine. With a little perseverance you will soon be knitting your first sweater. I remember my excitement on finishing my first garment. No need to discuss what it looked like, enough to say that I improved very quickly, helped by other knitters whose enthusiasm and knowledge were a real inspiration, and also by an insatiable curiosity to find out just how much my clever little machine would do.

The instruction book, however alien it may seem at first glance, will tell you all you need to know to make a start. It will explain most of the techniques your machine is capable of, but it may still leave you high and dry and wondering how you can put all these techniques together to make a sweater. A book of machine knitting patterns eagerly bought early on can also produce a feeling of baffled despair, and if you are used to a hand knitting pattern the technical terms will seem very strange. However, help is at hand. I hope in this book to help you to choose the right machine, to expand on the information you will find in your instruction book and to explain a few mysteries. It will show you how to use patterns, and above all – that great freedom – how to design for yourself.

Hazel

THE
MACHINE · KNITTER'S
HANDBOOK

HAZEL POPE

A DAVID & CHARLES CRAFT BOOK

ABBREVIATIONS

NWP	non-working position		
WP	working position		
UWP	upper working position		
HP	holding position		
N(s)	needle(s)		
L	left		
R	right		
carr	carriage	K	knit
st(s)	stitch(es)	MT	main tension
in	inch	FI	Fair Isle
cm	centimetre	rem	remain(ing)
MY	main yarn	beg	beginning
WY	waste yarn	EON	every other needle
r(s)	row(s)	RC	row counter
T	tension	alt	alternate(ly)

METRIC AND IMPERIAL APPROXIMATE EQUIVALENTS

Length

1cm	$\frac{3}{8}$in	71cm	28in
2cm	$\frac{3}{4}$in	76cm	30in
2.5cm	1in	84cm	33in
5cm	2in	89cm	35in
7.5cm	3in	94cm	37in
10cm	4in	99cm	39in
15cm	6in	104cm	41in
30.5cm	12in	109cm	43in
61cm	24in	112cm	44in

Weight

1kg	2lb 3$\frac{1}{2}$oz (2.2lb)
25gm	0.88oz
28.4gm	1oz

British Library Cataloguing in Publication Data

Pope, Hazel
   The machine knitters handbook.
   1. Machine knitting – Amateurs' manuals
   I. Title
   746.43'2

   ISBN 0-7153-9018-X

Typeset by Typesetters (Birmingham) Ltd,
Smethwick, West Midlands
Printed and bound in Italy
by New Interlitho
for David & Charles Publishers plc
Brunel House   Newton Abbot   Devon

Distributed in the United States by
Sterling Publishing Co, Inc,
2 Park Avenue, New York, NY 10016

CONTENTS

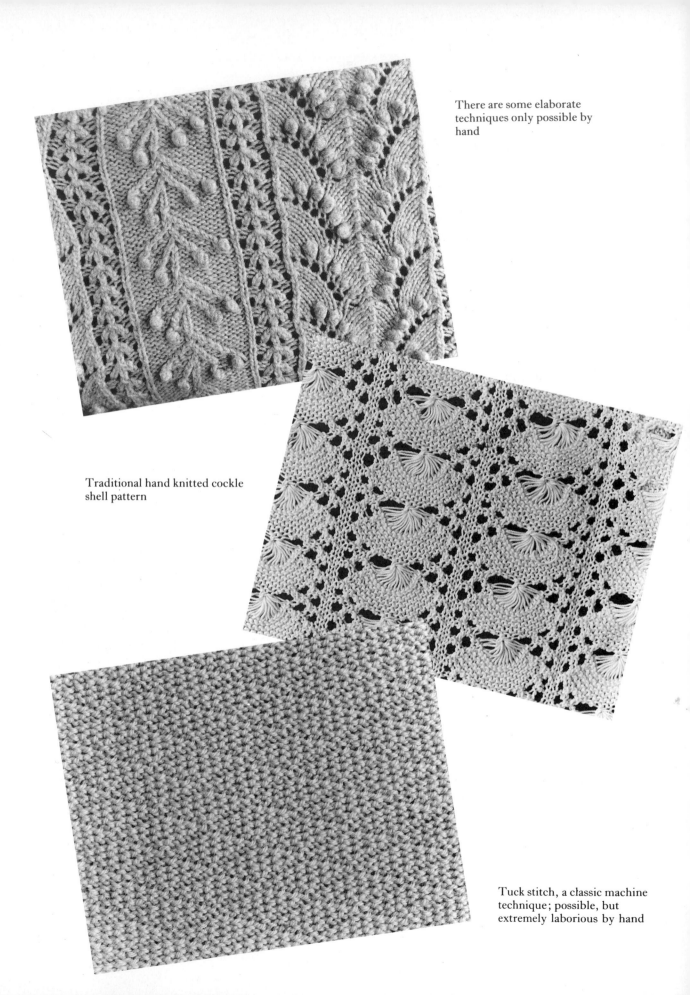

There are some elaborate techniques only possible by hand

Traditional hand knitted cockle shell pattern

Tuck stitch, a classic machine technique; possible, but extremely laborious by hand

1
UNDERSTANDING MACHINE·KNITTING

FIRST of all let's see what a machine will do that you can't do by hand and vice versa. Is mechanisation a good thing? The answer is not so much that it's good or bad, but that it's different.

A ball of wool and a pair of needles pop easily into a bag so that you can hand knit at any spare moment of the day – on the bus or the train, in your lunch hour, watching television or listening to the radio. However, a machine will need its own space, somewhere in the house where it can be left ready for action, and action means a considerable amount of noise. You won't be very popular if you're knitting where others are trying to enjoy more peaceful activities. You'll have to face up to the fact that machine knitting tends to be anti-social, except to other machine knitters. For these reasons many machine knitters who were originally hand knitters still enjoy hand knitting, developing their skills in stitch patterns and using yarns designed for hand knitting.

It is true to say that with a bit of compromise a machine can always produce patterns similar to hand knitting though you would need a chunky knitter to produce sweaters in some of the more exotic hand knitting yarns. Nowadays there is an enormous amount of luxury yarn developed for the machine, although it is generally only available in specialist shops and by mail order. If you do hand knit and feel that you are somehow being disloyal to the craft by thinking of buying a machine, you might decide that you will use the machine for the things it does best and reserve hand knitting for the more complex stitch patterns.

Of course the machine can be complex too, if you want it to be, although some of those complexities are simplified in the modern automatic machines. Remember that the machine is not imitating hand knitting, but producing stitches, textures and patterns of its own, some of which are based on hand knitting but many which are not. For example, the machine will not automatically knit combinations of garter stitch and lace as in many hand knitted Shetland patterns. What are called single bed machines will not produce a 'knit one, purl one rib', but can offer a very successful compromise. You need another

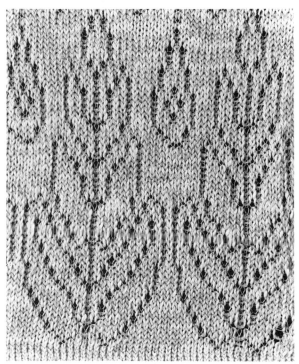

Unique to the machine, punch lace is a delicate and easy alternative to true lace

piece of machinery – a ribbing attachment – for a true rib.

The domestic knitting machine is similar in concept and function to those used in industry. It is sometimes called a 'hand flat', and you will hear terms such as 'single bed', 'double bed', and even 'true double bed' used. Very intriguing! As a beginner, the machine you will probably consider is a single bed machine. This means that you have only one needlebed and that the machine will only produce stockinet, or stocking stitch fabric, and pattern variations of this. As it knits, the 'wrong' or purl side of the knitting faces you. At first you may think this is very restricting, that you are going to have to hand knit ribs to garments or buy an extra attachment to produce a rib. Well, of course, you can do either of these but it must be emphasised that it is absolutely unnecessary as a compromise can be made either in garment design or by producing a mock rib, sometimes called an elastic hem or, to make it sound more exciting, continental rib.

Generally speaking, once you are knitting confidently, and your enthusiasm grows, you will probably want the option to produce a true rib. To do this you buy an attachment known as a ribber, which is simply another bed of needles which you set up facing your original machine giving you a double bed machine. The two sets of needles then work together to produce true ribbing for garment welts, and endless variations such as fisherman's rib at the simplest level, and at a more advanced and sophisticated level, beautiful jaquard fabric. The original single bed machine in this partnership is now known as the main or back bed. The ribbing attachment, or front bed, may be lowered and left on, or removed for single bed work. It only takes a few seconds to lower the bed, and a couple of minutes to remove it entirely should you wish to do so. The true double bed machine has both beds permanently set up as one unit. It produces excellent single bed work, but the delight of this kind of machine is the ease with which it produces beautiful ribbing and an endless variety of patterning on both beds. Some knitters would say that it is not really a machine to learn on, that one should have some experience of machine knitting using a single bed machine first. However it is certainly possible to start from scratch on these machines, and many knitters do.

Remember that you don't have to buy a simple machine just because you are a beginner, or because you eye machinery with mistrust and have no faith in your learning abilities. All modern machines have the basic knitting capacity which you will have to learn. To produce a pattern, and sometimes even to knit on the simplest machines, of which there are several on the market, much work has to be done by hand on the machine. The more sophisticated the machine becomes, the more the patterning techniques are automated.

I hope that the next chapter will help you to understand what sort of machine will suit your personal needs and temperament and to decide how automatically – in machine terms – adventurous you want to be. Remember too that no amount of technical potential on the machine's part, or technical ability on your part, can compare with an imaginative use of the machine. Many designers who knit for a living use old machines simply because they can't afford anything else, but are able to produce attractive, exciting garments. The machine is a means to an end, and though a designer may long to be able to afford the latest and most sophisticated machine, any restrictions an older model may present test their ingenuity and stimulate their imagination to produce well-designed garments within these restrictions. No amount of automatic wizardry will compensate for dreary or dreadful colour combinations, inferior yarn or bad garment design.

None of these confusing considerations put me off when I wanted a machine, and I am glad they didn't. I soon discovered that there's nothing to beat any automatic machine for producing, at its simplest, smooth, even-textured stocking stitch; Fair Isle patterns that aren't all puckered up; slip stitch and tuck stitch patterns that would take ages by hand; lovely, full lace designs in fine yarn and in a fine tension that would take a lifetime to knit by hand; complex-looking Fair Isle; picture sweaters; glistening evening sweaters; full skirts; coats; lengths of jersey fabric for dressmaking and all those childrens' clothes! Memories of hand knitting for me include garments which were outgrown before they were even finished – a Shetland shawl started for a first baby was finally completed in time for the third!

So it isn't a question of one method being better than the other; they are different. It's very cheap and easy to find out whether or not you like hand knitting. All you need is a pattern, yarn and needles, and little is lost if you decide you don't enjoy it. Not so with machine knitting where a mistake can be expensive, even if you buy a second-hand machine. The next chapter will help you not to waste your money.

· The disabled knitter ·

It's very important, if you are disabled in any way, to know how mobile you need to be to use a machine. If you are registered disabled, or have a minor disability which restricts certain movements, it is a sound idea to watch someone using a machine. Not just for five minutes, but long enough to take in all the movements required for various techniques, and to observe what the knitter has to do when things go wrong. Simple things like weights dropping to the floor, cones of yarn falling over, tangles of yarn in the tension mast, have to be considered. You know the scope of your own mobility and watching someone else at work will help you to apply this to using a machine. If you spend most of your time in a wheelchair, are you able to retrieve fallen equipment? Can you reach up to thread the tension mast? Perhaps you could adapt the

The Simpleframe is ideal for those with restricted mobility

mast to remove from its socket to thread up – an easier solution than it sounds.

Above all you will need to consider whether you will be able to have your machine set up somewhere where there is plenty of space around it, allowing you freedom of movement. You will have to go around behind it to put cones of yarn on the floor, and change these when necessary.

· Are you sitting comfortably? ·

Many of us have a physical restriction of some sort, and are to varying degrees incapacitated by things like bad backs, stiff necks and other such gloomy aches and pains of a temporary or permanent nature. These can make themselves apparent when sitting for a length of time concentrating on any physically limited activity which creates tension in specific areas of the body.

Your common sense, related to your own particular problem, should dictate how you sit at your machine, and for how long. Much better to work for an hour, get up and have a stretch, then continue knitting, than to crouch over the machine for several hours – time passes quickly when you are absorbed by something – and stagger away unable to carry on. Your sitting position can be adjusted and supported by cushions or, if you can afford it, with a specially designed chair. So make sure you sit properly and rest every so often, particularly when you are learning. Determination to master the machine can disperse all other thoughts and find you stiff and bad tempered after several hours of concentration!

If you have shoulder or arm problems, you could consider 'motorising' your machine. This means that the carriage is driven for you electrically, leaving only techniques such as casting on and off and shaping to be done by hand.

Sitting comfortably; the machine knitter in the workshop

2
YOUR·FIRST·MACHINE

AS a newcomer to machine knitting you will probably find yourself bewildered by the confusing array of machines on the market. You know that you want a knitting machine, but how do you decide which machine you want? The first thing to consider is the main uses you intend to put your machine to.

For a hobby Then you need a versatile machine because you are going to make the time and have the motivation to explore all the possibilities of a fully-automatic machine with all its creative potential. Your hobby will quickly develop as your knitting horizons expand.

For family knitting You may think you only need a simple machine to do basic practical sweaters for school, sport and work, but it's marvellous to have the potential in the machine for automatic decoration. Young children in particular love picture sweaters, their name in bright letters across their chest, or a single motif of a favourite animal. As your confidence and ability grow you will appreciate the advantages of an automatic machine. Don't underestimate your capabilities and don't let the fact that you may have 'never been any good with mechanical things' deter you.

To earn a living Again you will find any of the simpler machines very limiting. If you are knitting for friends or neighbours, or for your own stall in a local market, you will not want to hear yourself say 'I'm sorry, but I can't do that on my machine'. Knitwear designers often advertise in the specialist machine knitting magazines for experienced knitters. It may take a little time before you have the confidence to call yourself experienced, but you would never be able to cope with much of the intricate and interesting work offered on anything less than a fully-automatic machine.

· What sort of machine do you want? ·

Apart from being 'basic' or 'automatic', machines fall into distinct categories according to the thickness of yarn they use. The term 'gauge' is used to refer to the thickness of the needles on the machine and the distance between them.

Standard gauge single bed machines 200 needles. Gauge 4.5mm.

These machines will knit yarns as fine as sewing cotton, through a range of 2, 3 and 4 ply equivalent yarns up to 5 ply Guernsey. In addition, yarn of double knitting weight can be knitted successfully by using every other needle. Obviously it is unlikely that you would knit a sweater in sewing cotton, but there are exciting techniques you can work on the machine using yarns of this weight in combination with thicker yarns.

Wide gauge single bed machines 110, 114 or 115 needles, according to model. Gauge 8mm or 9mm.

Often known as chunky machines, wide gauge machines will knit double knitting weight and all yarns thicker than this. There is an enormous choice of yarns in this range, including mohair and thick bouclé.

Fine gauge machines 250 needles. Gauge 3.6mm.

These are more specialised machines, designed for fine knitting in anything from sewing cotton up to 4 ply equivalent.

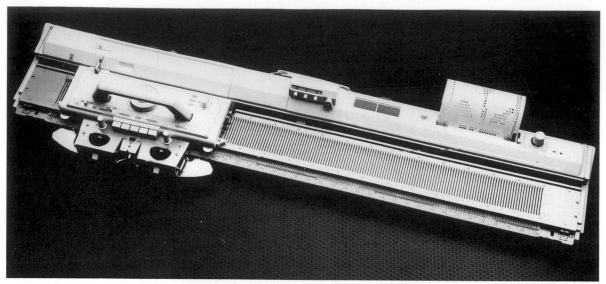

(*this page and top opposite*)
The choice is yours; a
selection of single bed
machines

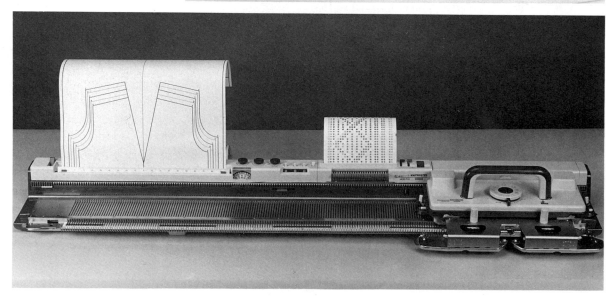

(*above*) The Bond keeps the
balance between hand and
machine knitting; (*right*) the
chunky machine happily knits
thick and textured yarns

Double bed machines 180 needles on each bed. Gauge 5mm.
These are standard gauge machines with two needle beds set up as one unit. There is a facility to lower the front bed when required.

· The Simpleframe and the Bond ·

Anyone who is particularly hesitant about going mechanised might like to give consideration to these two somewhat different wide gauge machines. They bridge the gap between hand knitting and machine knitting, and produce work which compares so well with hand knitting that it is virtually impossible to spot the difference. They are lightweight to use, the Bond needs only a table or an ironing board as its support, while the Simpleframe is even more amenable and can be worked on your knee.

The big attraction of these two devices is the price – you can become mechanised for much less than the price of a chunky machine, with which they most nearly compare. If for some reason your creative urge far outweighs your practical capability, and impatience to achieve results precludes the learning process using needles and yarn, then you will quickly learn and achieve results on either of these.

The Simpleframe 96 needles. Gauge 7mm.
The Simpleframe is not exactly a machine, but a frame on which the knitting can be worked without the degree of concentration required for other machines. Therapeutic, it is quietly operated without the mechanical rattle which banishes most machine knitters to solitary confinement. Small and neat as it is, it still gives a double bed facility, having 48 needles on each side of the frame, a total of 96. Each stitch is worked manually after the yarn has been laid across the needles.

The same method of making the stitch applies to the new 100 needle single bed model. Resting easily across the arms of an easy chair or a wheelchair, the S100 is easy to work single handed, further recommendations to those of us with restricted mobility or disability.

The Bond 100 needles. Gauge 8mm.
The Bond, which boasts a Design Centre Award, is also less demanding on space and noise tolerance, but once supplemented with its ever growing number of accessories it begins to lose its original simplicity. There are 100 needles in the bed, with an extension kit of 30 extra needles available if required. The knitting action is achieved by laying the yarn across the needles by hand and the stitches are then knitted when you move the carriage over them.

It is possible to work a great variety of manual stitch patterns on these 'machines', using chunky yarns to produce luxury garments. It soon becomes a simple matter to adapt hand knitting patterns and all the lovely fashion yarns, from double knitting thickness to the chunkiest of fancy yarns, are workable. Practise at first with bits and pieces left over from hand knitting, or buy a selection of interesting textures and thicknesses from an oddments box before spending on a luxury yarn for your first garment.

Even though they are worked manually, the Bond and the Simpleframe become easy and quick to use with practice. However, you can't expect the resultant knitting to grow quite so rapidly as it does on a true machine. Both of these devices provide an alternative to the technical sophistication of the modern knitting machine and may be just the compromise that some knitters require.

· Further considerations ·

The next decision you have to make is whether you require an automatic or a non-automatic machine, and if you decide on automatic you then have a further choice between punchcard machines and electronic machines. Undoubtedly you will find all this very difficult to understand at first. Remember that there are two stages of learning on a knitting machine. The first stage involves learning the basic knitting techniques (casting on and off, increasing and decreasing etc) independent of pattern and is common to all machines. The second stage, in which you learn to produce stitch patterns according to your machine's capability, is much easier since you are building on your basic experience and your growing familiarity with machine knitting.

Non-automatic machines Any patterning has to be done manually on these machines. Unless you are completely convinced that you only want a knitting machine in order to be able to run up basic sweaters at high speed, then I would recommend that you make an automatic model your minimum requirement.

Semi-automatic machines There are a number of machines at the less expensive end of the range which are termed semi-automatic. Some of these have punchcards in combination with selector buttons for patterning, some have selector buttons only. Although the basic techniques are as easy on these machines as on any other, considerable manual effort is required to produce stitch patterns. Many of the models which fall into this category are now obsolete, but you may well come across them if you are buying second-hand.

Punchcard machines These automatic machines will produce patterned fabric when a pattern card is introduced and the machine is set up according to the stitch required. The cards have punched holes which allow needles to be selected for patterning, and it is very simple to design and punch pattern cards yourself. On most machines the maximum repeat is 24 stitches and 60 rows. The needles are selected either in the bed of the machine or by the carriage. Try both types of machine to see which method you prefer.

Electronic machines These machines are computerised, so you need to be able to plug them into a power supply in order to obtain stitch patterns. They have both simplified and extended automatic patterning on the knitting machine and can also be programmed for some other knitting features. One model boasts 555 stitch patterns stored in its memory – you simply key in the number and the pattern is

Computers incorporate a wide range of programmes; put in your information and they tell you what to do and when to do it (see page 20)

The electronic machine reads the black squares on the sheet but, unlike the punched cards, can then be programmed from one repeat unit according to your needs. The card width is 60 stitches as opposed to 24 for most standard machines, 40 for Pfaff/Passap

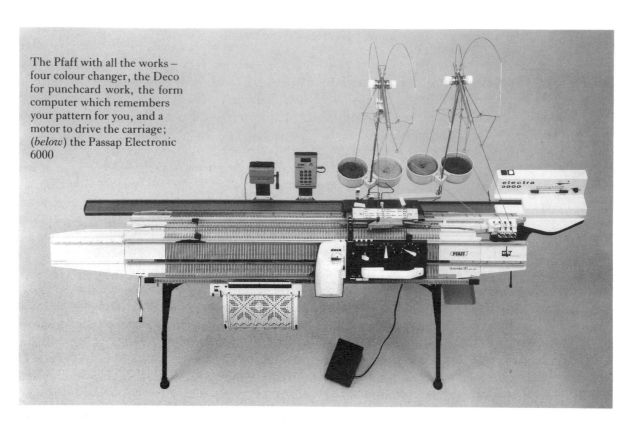

The Pfaff with all the works –
four colour changer, the Deco
for punchcard work, the form
computer which remembers
your pattern for you, and a
motor to drive the carriage;
(*below*) the Passap Electronic
6000

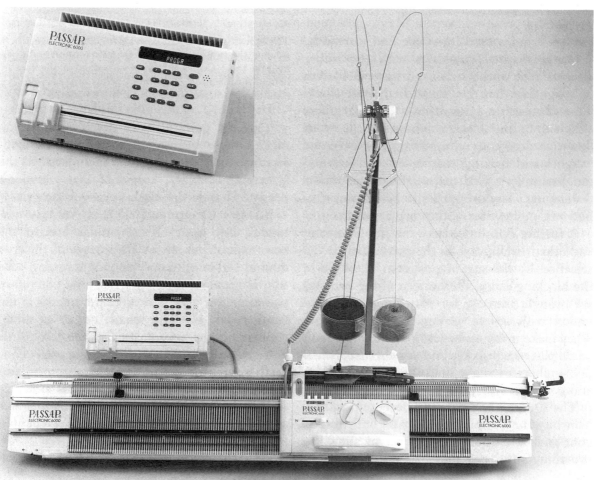

extra available is the transfer lock, which enables you to transfer stitches from double bed to single bed knitting almost as quickly as knitting a row, saving the laborious process of hand transfer with a double-ended bodkin. It also makes lace patterns and garter stitch effects possible.

Fully-automatic patterning comes with the purchase of the Deco. This pattern system gives a 40 stitch repeat facility, and is in two parts; the card reader, which fits onto a slotted rack at the bottom of the front bed, and the selector which rides along the upper and lower guide rail on the front bed and is easily coupled to the lock when in use. It is the Deco which may be the major influence on your decision between any of the single beds and the Duomatic. Remember that the Duomatic is primarily a double bed machine, and that as such the Fair Isle work produced has no floats or strands at the back of the work. In their eagerness to get rid of floats at the back of the work, beginners may want to knit double bed Fair Isle bands on a stocking stitch sweater. This would give unsatisfactory results as the difference in tension and thickness of the resultant fabric makes this combination unsuitable so the Fair Isle patterning would also have to be single bed work. Since the Deco mechanism selects the pattern every two rows, then any single bed Fair Isle pattern will have a two row repeat and would need to be designed accordingly, which could be restricting on small areas.

The pattern books produced for the Duomatic show how versatile the machine is, both in patterning and in its ability to use fancy yarns, though it is important to remember that it is happiest using finer yarns when knitting double bed Fair Isle. My first attempts at using the Deco attachment with Shetland yarn produced delightful patterns, but the work was more like corrugated cardboard than the soft fabric one expects of knitting. This was simply remedied by using a fine 2 ply equivalent yarn. Further experiments with industrial angora and lambswool produced a lovely light fabric, the angora texture revealed when the sample was washed.

Many extras can be added to the Duomatic to increase its versatility and to speed up the knitting process. It all seems a very expensive exercise, but if you need to make basic financial comparisons, your arithmetic for the single bed must include the price of ribber, a two colour changer and a table, to form a true comparison with the Duomatic plus Deco.

Lighter weight than the Pfaff/Passap machines, the Singer double bed machine more nearly approaches the single bed machine with ribbing attachment. The work needs weighting in the same way. Patterning is electronic, and the carriage can be motor driven

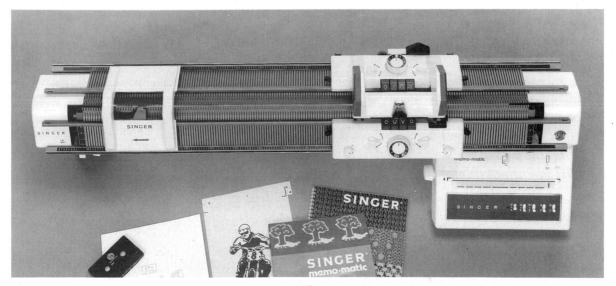

· The Singer double bed machines ·

Singer have recently come back into the market with two true double bed machines. These are both electronic – the pattern is either drawn on a programme grid or onto a special sheet of paper, and the needles are selected electronically. Although they are much lighter in weight than the Duomatics they are nevertheless very sturdy. Singer have made these machines look very up-to-date in design, with simple, bold, easy-to-understand symbols on the carriage and bed. The bed itself is constructed from anti-glare metal. On these machines it is necessary to hang weights on the work as for single bed machines with a separate ribber.

In a perfect world where there's endless time for knitting and money is no object, an automatic single bed standard machine, an automatic chunky machine and a Duomatic could satisfy the requirements and desires of the most obsessive machine knitter. The Singer machines fill a gap between the standard electronic single bed machine plus ribber and the Duomatics. Whichever machine you finally decide upon, it will give you a lot of satisfaction and enjoyment.

· Additional equipment ·

If you are in possession of a knitting machine and some yarn then you are adequately equipped to knit; however, one or two extras do make life a little easier. The order of importance of the larger attachments and accessories is a matter of personal choice, but the first two listed below are ones which you might like to add to your initial outlay. There are many other attachments and accessories to tempt you and if you become an enthusiastic knitter you are bound to want to budget for some of them. Experience will help you to decide which of the accessories on offer will be of value to you.

Knitting table Fixed to this, your machine can be left set up and ready to use at any time. Cones or prepared balls of yarn can be placed on the floor behind the table which is the most efficient way of supplying yarn to the machine. This, as well as more obvious domestic reasons, make having a purpose-built knitting table infinitely preferable to setting the machine up on your dining table.

Wool winder This is essential for winding off amounts of yarn for machine knitting, especially if it is not supplied on cones, as you cannot knit on a machine from a hand-wound ball. There are several kinds on the market to choose from.

The electric yarn winder; electrified winding is quick, but there are plenty of hand winders on the market

Charting device This accessory dispenses with the need for detailed pattern instructions. The shape of your garment is drawn onto a pattern sheet and the device is set up in such a way that it indicates the number of stitches to cast on, where to increase and decrease and how many rows to knit. It either fits onto the back of your machine or may be incorporated in it, according to the model.

Knitting pattern computer Some manufacturers produce small computers which can be attached to the back of their machines. You key in your pattern information and the computer does the calculations for you, flashing up pattern instructions as you knit.

Ribbing attachment Once you have become familiar with a single bed machine this may well be the first addition you want to make to your equipment, particularly if you already have a built-in charting device. It not only

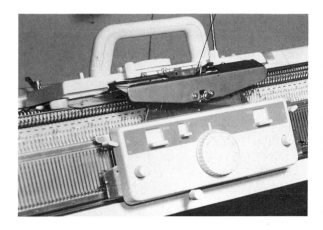

The ribbing attachment

The Brother transfer carriage – much easier to use than it looks – saves time if you own a ribber

enables you to knit ribbed welts, but also to use varieties of ribbed patterns – fisherman's rib for example – for whole garments.

Transfer carriage Once you have a ribber this accessory is invaluable. With it stitches can be transferred from one bed to another in one easy movement instead of having to be painstakingly transferred manually, stitch by stitch. It can also be used to increase the variety of stitch patterns that you can produce.

Intarsia carriage A separate carriage for automatic machines which enables you to knit pictures and other designs that cannot be worked automatically.

Garter carriage This works on the single bed of some Brother machines to produce the garter stitch familiar to hand knitters. By introducing a pattern card to the machine the carriage can also knit garter stitch patterns

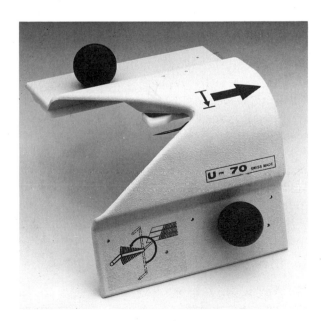

The U70 transfer lock for Duomatic machines transfers stitches from double bed rib ready for single bed work in seconds; it also increases stitch pattern potential

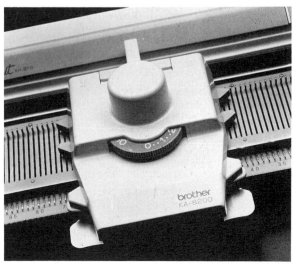

The intarsia carriage opens up possibilities for free design without the restriction of card size; sometimes the facility is built in. A must for picture knitting

such as those on traditional fisherman's ganseys, for example. It will also knit rib. Motorised, it chugs along unattended, stopping only if there is an obstruction or if it is programmed to do so.

Linker This accessory automates the casting-off process, replacing manual casting off using the latch tool.

Colour changers These are available as extras for single bed machines and single bed machines with ribber attached, but they are standard on the Pfaff and Passap double bed machines as they are an integral part of this system of knitting. Up to four colours can be set up in feeding eyelets, which are then picked up automatically by the carriage as necessary. At its most basic a colour changer means that you can knit stripes without the bother of changing the yarn in the feeder, while at a more advanced level it can be used for Fair Isle patterns, and in conjunction with a ribber it will enable you to knit in the floats or loops at the back of this type of work.

Garter bar This is a metal bar which looks like an enormous multi-transfer tool. It enables you to turn your knitting round on the machine without knitting it onto waste yarn, turning it and replacing it stitch by stitch onto the needles. Although it seems clumsy to use at first, you will soon become adept with practice. If you are not going to use it very much it is an expensive alternative to waste yarn, and if you want to knit a lot of garter stitch patterns it would probably be better to save up for a garter carriage – make sure you buy a machine which takes this attachment.

Motor A motor can be attached to some machines to relieve you of the task of driving the carriage.

Punch This enables you to punch out your own designs onto purchased blank cards for automatic punchcard machines. It is unnecessary for electronic machines.

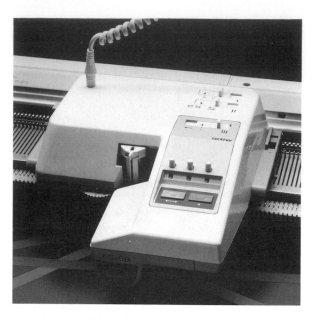

The garter carriage. Most Brother machines now take this optional and amazing accessory; apart from garter stitch patterns it also enables you to knit ribs without a ribber

The linker makes casting off with the latch tool a thing of the past

Pattern cards Blanks are available for both automatic and electronic machines on which you can execute your own designs or duplicate those found in books or magazines. Each manufacturer produces sets of designs ready for you to punch or draw out onto purchased cards.

· Buying a machine ·

The preceding information should have helped to give you a clearer idea of the sort of knitting machine that you are looking for, but you still have to make a decision about which model to buy. Before making your choice, read as much literature as you can from manufacturers and, better still, talk to experienced knitters. You are bound to become confused since there are several manufacturers in the market, each one producing a variety of machines at any one time. Most adult education centres hold classes in machine knitting and a good tutor will let you 'sit in' so that you can see a variety of different machines in action. There are machine knitting clubs all over the world full of enthusiastic knitters only too willing to help and encourage the beginner. Specialist shops can put you in touch with these and are often very helpful too, hopeful of course to sell you a machine!

Amidst this ocean of information, it may be some comfort to know that all the single bed machines in production, including the chunky machines, are of a comparable quality and will give you equally good service. However advanced they may be technically, the methods for casting on, casting off, increasing and decreasing are all the same (unless the machine has a cast-on comb which gives an extra method, not a basic difference). They then part company in the method of needle selection for stitch patterns, which will be indicated in the machine guide. Let me emphasise that one method is not better than the other, it's simply a question of personal choice, so one machine is going to be no more difficult to learn on than another. It's as well to try out machines of both types to get the feel of the

knitting carriage under your hand, to help you make your own decision.

The true double bed machine has a completely different method of needle selection from a single bed and for many stitch patterns needs no card. It does need more concentration and perseverance in the initial learning stage, which aficionados of these machines would deem well worth while.

The information in the table at the end of this chapter gives a comprehensive guide to all the machines available in the United Kingdom. It is correct at the time of writing, but as with everything else in our consumer society, competition dictates a continuous striving for improvement. New models appear at fairly regular intervals, though on the whole earlier accesories will also adapt to these. Make sure when you buy a machine that all the current gadgets produced by the same firm will suit your model. At this stage you may not think that you will ever need them, but you will probably be surprised how your ideas will alter as you master your machine. It is most important when buying second-hand to find out if you will be able to obtain attachments for your purchase. No such problems present themselves with true double bed machines. The basic machine is constant – it does not become obsolete and is not superseded by a better or different model. As new ideas develop, they are adapted onto the basic machine. This means that you can start with whatever you think you can afford and add extras as you go along without worrying that any of your purchases will become out of date.

When choosing a machine, whether new or second-hand, have a list of questions you want to ask ready. If you are looking at a single bed machine these might include:

Can I add a ribber?
Can I add a charting device?
Can I add an intarsia carriage?
Can I knit true lace designs?
Can I knit patterns in thicker yarns?

Of course if you are buying an old machine to learn on, simply to find out whether or not you like machine knitting, some of these questions might not be relevant for you.

Second-hand machines This is probably the cheapest way to buy, providing the machine is in good condition. Make sure it is a model for which important attachments such as ribber, charting device, intarsia carriage etc are still currently on the market – you may want to add them later. When you go to look at a second-hand machine it should be set up in working position for you to see it in action. However, it often happens that the person selling it doesn't know how to use it and neither do you! It is a very good idea to find an experienced knitter to go with you, who will know what to look for, recognise damage and notice missing parts. However if you are on your own, check that the needlebed is not damaged, that there are no dents in the needle slots and the sinkers are not bent. Take the carriage off the bed and twiddle all the knobs whilst watching the mechanism underneath. Everything you twiddle should produce a movement – if it doesn't then it is broken and no use to you.

I bought my first machine – a second-hand Knitmaster 321 – through an advert in the local paper. I had telephoned Knitmaster, worried that I might be wasting a precious £50, and they put me in touch with one of their tutors, who subsequently came with me to vet the machine.

It had hardly been used and was extremely stiff. A few drops of oil soon had the carriage knitting smoothly over 200 needles, all the automatic patterning techniques were tried, and the machine pronounced perfect. I taught myself to knit on it and knitted enthusiastically almost every day for five years. I eventually added a second-hand ribber, but it was not quite such a good buy as the original purchase. It was an obsolete model, which though it knitted beautifully, did not drop down from the main bed as far as the later models. That,

of course, was why it was for sale.

After a while I began to yearn to knit lacy things and at the time the Brother machine offered this facility, so I traded my machine and ribber for a nearly-new Brother 840, eventually adding a new ribber, charting device and an intarsia carriage. I am still waiting to treat myself to a transfer carriage and a linker.

Initially I wasn't sure whether I would like machine knitting and a secondhand machine seemed the best way to find out. I was fortunate enough to buy a good one. Remember though, that second-hand purchases do constitute a risk and you have no guarantee against defect.

Buying a new machine By far the best way to buy a new machine is from your nearest specialist shop. It is very easy to find favourable prices in catalogues and from postal suppliers who may be many miles from your home area, but should anything go wrong you may well be very disappointed in the after-sales service, if one exists. Your local machine knitting shop, on the other hand, is very keen for your continued trade and should not let you down. The shop is staffed by enthusiasts who will help you with your teething problems and can put you in touch with other knitters, with clubs, classes, courses and conventions. A wise shopkeeper will let you spend hours looking at machines and asking questions. Even if you go away and buy a second-hand machine he is still going to benefit from your custom in yarn purchase and the attachments you will want to buy later on.

The machines mentioned in this book are available worldwide, but outside the United Kingdom some makes are distributed by different companies. For example, the Knitmaster machine you buy in the United Kingdom is in Australia under the Singer label. Your stockist will help you if any queries arise.

SINGLE BED MACHINES

Automatic Machines	Basic Machine	Lace Carriage	Lace Carriage and Charting Device	Charting Device	Intarsia	Ribbing Attachment – separate	Remarks
KNITMASTER	Needle selection in carriage	Single action. Remove yarn for transfer.		Knitradar – paper sheets ½ and full scale			Standard gauge machines have 200 Ns
Standard gauge punchcard	260K Zippy de luxe	260KL 600KL 700KL	700KL	360K 700K 700KL	600K 700K 600KL 700KL	SRP60 for 600s, 700s and Zippy de luxe	All attachments available for 260K and Zippy de luxe
Standard gauge electronic	SK550	SK560			AG20 for all standard machines	SRP50	60st repeat
Fine gauge punchcard	FK270	FKL270	FKL370	KR7 for FK 270		FRP70	250 needles
Chunky – no punchcard	151					SR150	110 needles
Chunky – punchcard	155					SR155	110 needles. 24st pattern repeat
Chunky	Zippy 90			Separate non-attachable accessory			Basic manual 90 needle machine
TOYOTA	Needle selector in machine bed			Knit Tracer Full scale, ½ width transparent sheet		Ribber only takes Simulknit	Simulknit for reversible fair isle
Standard gauge semi-automatic		Transfers only / KS858		K33A	K82A	505	12st pattern repeat. Lever selects needles
Standard gauge punchcard		KS901		K33A	K82A	501	24st pattern repeat
Standard gauge punchcard		KS958		K33A	K82A	506	24st pattern repeat
JONES/BROTHER	Needle selection in machine bed	Transfers only		Knit Leader Full scale, full width transparent sheet			
Standard gauge punchcard	KH836	KA836 KH890	KH881 KH891	KL116 for KH-836 KH881 KH891	KA8200 for KH836 KA8210	KR830 for 836 KR850 for all others	Electronic garter carriage available
Standard gauge electronic	KH910 KH950	KH910 KH950 'Electroknit'		KL116 for all models without built-in device	KA8200 for KH910 KH950	KR850	KH950: 555 in-built patterns 60st repeat and variations
Chunky – no punchcard	KH230			KL116	KH230	KR260	114 needles
Chunky automatic	KH260			KL116	KA2600	KR260	114 needles
SINGER	Electronic needle selection on automat c			Pattern Driver Full scale – half width			Computer available – simplifies calculations
Single bed electronic	Memo II 400		One mode only		SB100	400 converts to double bed Memo 11/600	Electronic 16×16 grid extendable repeat on 400
Standard gauge non-automatic	SB100						
Chunky – no punchcard	Designer 2				Intarsia facility		115 needles
BOND	Manual machine. One model only				Intarsia facility	One model only	Simple machine 100 needles
PFAFF	Monomatic		Forma ½ scale				Identical machines. Pushers built in for manual patterning
PASSAP	SB20		Forma ½ scale				Automatic 2 col. changer

Machines are listed under their built-in facilities. Any shaded section shows facility is not built in, and gives the reference number of the attachment. These are basic requirements only, there are many other accessories and attachments. Knitmaster, Toyota and Jones/Brother are Japanese machines. Singer is manufactured in France, Bond is British. Passap and Pfaff are identical Swiss machines.

TRUE DOUBLE BED MACHINES

PASSAP/PFAFF Model	Description	Remarks
Duomatic 80 (80H-2)	Double-bed, 2 colour changer and stand	No weights required. Pusher system gives facility for manual patterning. Colour can be changed automatically.
Duomatic 80 (80H-4)	As above but with a 4 colour changer	Any 2 of 4 colours can be changed automatically. 3rd or 4th can be pre-selected.
Duomatic 80 (80C-2)	As for 80H-2 but with Deco automatic fairisle	40 st pattern repeat Fair Isle is knitted 2 rows background and 2 rows contrast.
Duomatic 80 (80C-4)	As for 80C-2 but with 4 colour changer	This is the most popular combination (in the U.K.)
MOTORS M-3000A M-75B	Lightweight motor Heavy duty motor	For occasional use For professional use
Accessory ZII	Count-down, colour change programme and yarn-break cut out. Has to be purchased already built-in to either of the motors	Cuts off after pre-selected number of rows up to 9999. Can change any 2 pre-selected colours at every 2nd row, up to every 20 rows.
Passap Electronic 6000	Double-bed, 4 colour changer and stand	Similar bed to Duomatic. Needles, stitch patterns and techniques selected electronically. The Form Computer is built into the programming console.

The Forma charting device and Form Computer (for knitting calculations) fit all machines. At the time of writing, the Passap Electronic is not yet on the market, so a check should be made on applying existing accessories when purchasing.

SINGER		
Standard gauge double bed Memo II 600	Electronic patterning on a 16×16 programme. Grid charting device (Pattern Driver) and transfer carriage available. Computer simplifies calculations and knitting (separate accessory). Weights required.	
2310	Electronic patterning on a 60st repeat sheet. As above.	

(Passap is the original brand name marketed in the U.K. by Bogod Machine Co. Pfaff is an identical machine marketed in the U.K. by Pfaff GB Ltd. Singer is manufactured in France.)

3
MAKING·A·START

*I*N some ways it could be an advantage never to have used knitting needles; hand knitting can leave a legacy of hang-ups where a machine is concerned. Not only does the new terminology come as a shock, but so does the realisation that there is still a considerable amount of hand work necessary in machine knitting. However, as you study your instruction book you will begin to forget your presuppositions and to think in the idiom of the machine. And as you learn to use the tools necessary for the various hand techniques you will quickly become adept. And as your interest quickens, the whole process of knitting on the machine will become speedy and satisfying.

· What does it all mean? ·

With my first machine, a second-hand Knitmaster 321, I inherited a pile of pattern books. I had seen the machine in action – it all looked so easy! So the first thing I did was to choose a pattern, a striped sweater with puffed sleeves. I began to read it through. The more I read, the more apprehensive I became. How I would ever apply what I was reading to the machine in front of me – which I now saw had the tension mast set in upside down – I could not think. I had at least remembered vaguely how the machine had been set up! But what was MT? Whatever was waste yarn? After I had capitulated and decided it wasn't going to be possible to knit a sweater before tea-time and that I ought myself to observe the patience I expect of others, I managed to follow the instruction book, to cast on, and to knit a few inches. To my horror it was back to front, the purl side facing me! I promptly 'phoned Knitmaster to find out what was wrong. The embarrassed silence at the other end of the telephone indicated that I must be asking a silly question. In fact in all my years teaching no-one has ever asked me anything quite so ludicrous. I can only excuse myself by saying that it was quite a while before I accepted the difference between hand and machine knitting, and I was initially rather hampered by expecting machine knitting to be the same, only faster! I had never been good with machines of any sort, and found the drawings and diagrams baffling.

I was determined to master the problem, and after a week of practising every evening, I did follow the pattern I had chosen. I had learned what waste yarn was, and MT, and a lot more besides. From the size of the garment, I obviously hadn't learned just how important tension was, but it was a mistake I never made again.

· The instruction book ·

With every machine there is an instruction book. If you buy second-hand and the book is missing make sure it is still obtainable – your local stockist should be able to help here.

One hears much criticism of these books. Some are certainly better presented than others, none pretend to be more than a basic manual. They are for the most part logical and clear, and tell the beginner everything necessary to make a start. But there are so many things to learn at once – all the accessories are strange and seem to have weird names. It seems a lot to learn just to produce a simple piece of knitting, but try to relate it to something else you have learned which you now do quickly, without thinking about the mechanics of it. Can you remember learning to use scissors, tie shoelaces, thread-up and use a sewing machine, drive a car? Imagine trying to write instructions for any of these functions – it would be quite a problem to make them appear the simple actions they become with practice.

So bear this in mind when you look at the first technique your instruction book endeavours to teach you, which is plain knitting. In one of the manuals the instructions for this occupy four pages and need 26 informative pictures. Once you have followed these, step by step, several times, it will only take you a minute to perform, so persevere, it is far less complicated than it looks. Whilst you are learning how to produce this piece of knitting you are also getting the feel of the machine. Often everything goes wrong at once – have patience, you learn a lot from these early mistakes.

· How the machine works ·

From the machines illustrated in this book and those which you see in the shops, you will notice that all machines consist of three main parts, which when working together in harmony, produce perfect knitting.

The needlebed The needles lie in slots in the bed of the machine. They are separated from each other when working by the sinkers which are at the front of the bed.

The knitting carriage In order to knit, the carriage has to be passed over the needles with yarn in the yarn feeder. The front of the carriage has a detachable section known as the sinker plate.

The yarn tension unit The yarn is supplied to the feeder on the carriage by a piece of equipment which slots into position at the back of the bed. This is known as the yarn break or yarn mast.

The yarn mast has a tension unit incorporated. Through this the yarn passes and is controlled before being taken down through the yarn feeder on the carriage. This tension unit could be said to correspond to the control that is exercised in hand knitting by the hand not engaged in the knitting action – generally the left hand. Yarn tension control here affects the way in which the yarn is fed to the machine, and must be regulated according to its thickness and texture. You soon get used to adjusting this, because it affects the edges of your knitting. When the carriage jams it is often a result of lack of control at the top, so to speak.

The carriage sits on the rails of the needlebed. When moved along the bed it can be set to activate any needles in working position. The yarn is now brought down through the yarn feeder at the front of the carriage which when moved across the bed supplies yarn to the needles, thus forming a stitch. The size of this stitch is controlled by a numbered tension dial on the carriage and will be governed by the thickness and texture of the yarn and also by the feel you want your finished garment to have. The tension dial on the carriage controlling the stitch corresponds to needle size in hand knitting.

· The needle positions ·

There are four needle positions marked on the bed. The reference markings often differ from one machine to another, but the positions are the same on all single bed machines, and their optional ribbing attachments. When you first start to knit you are only concerned with two positions: non-working position (NWP) – the needles are pushed right to the back of the bed and are out of action – and working position (WP), which is the second position from the back. In this position the needles will knit when the carriage is passed over them. The third position from the back of the bed is known as upper working position (UWP), and when the needles are brought right out to the front of the bed as far as they will go they are said to be in holding position (HP).

· Holding position ·

Holding position is one of the most versatile needle positions. It has endless uses, both

The single bed machine

The yarn mast. The flow of yarn from the cone or ball behind the machine is controlled on its journey to the yarn feeder at the front of the carriage by the tension disc, and the take-up spring on the yarn mast

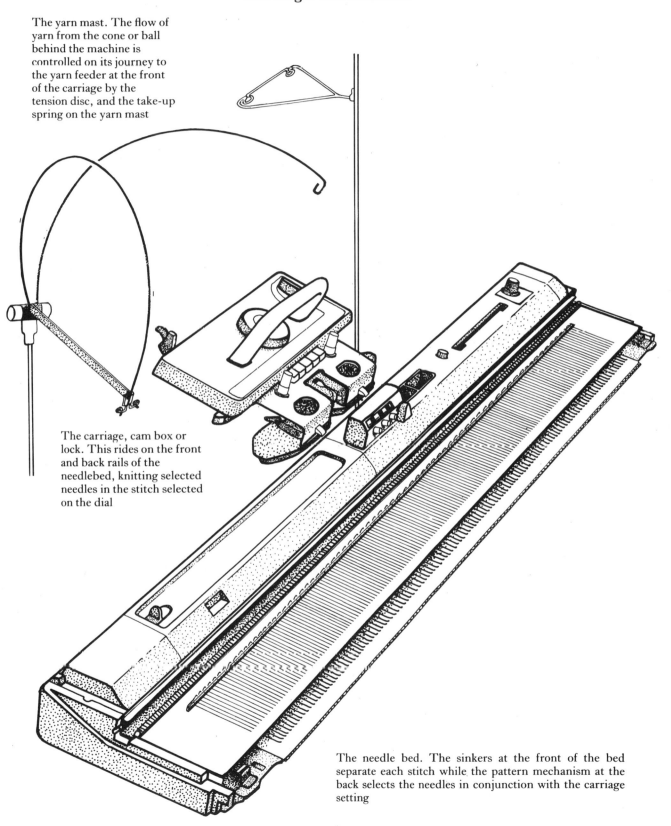

The carriage, cam box or lock. This rides on the front and back rails of the needlebed, knitting selected needles in the stitch selected on the dial

The needle bed. The sinkers at the front of the bed separate each stitch while the pattern mechanism at the back selects the needles in conjunction with the carriage setting

utilitarian and decorative. Understanding the many uses of this needle position is one of the fundamentals of machine knitting, and can speed up the knitting process. The required needles are brought right out to the front of the bed. The carriage is set to hold, and will then only knit those needles in working position. The needles that were brought out to the front of the bed don't knit. Set the carriage back to normal knitting, and they will knit back to working position. Also practise pushing needles back to upper working position, they will knit whether the carriage is on normal or hold. Try this without any yarn in the machine until you accustom yourself to setting the carriage, and begin to relate the setting to the needle action.

Holding position with the carriage set to hold is used for partial knitting or 'short-row shaping' at necklines, the bottom of skirts and dresses and full gathered sleeves, for flares in sideways knitted skirts, and for decorative colour effects on sweaters and jackets. It is also very useful when casting on by hand where it is impossible to use weights for the first few rows. By pulling the needles out to holding position on each row, but setting the carriage to normal knitting, the stitches will knit back to working position. Once there is enough knitting to gain a purchase, you can hang the weights onto the work. Holding position will be dealt with in more detail in Chapter 6.

· The weights ·

Most single bed machines come supplied with two claw weights which are quite adequate for most work. Weighting the work keeps the stitches firmly in the needles, very necessary when you are using lightweight yarns, a springy yarn such as pure wool, or you are working stitch patterns where the needles have a lot of work to do, as in tuck stitch and true lace designs. Lack of adequate weighting is often the cause of the machine not knitting properly.

Certain yarns may present knitting problems which are solved by simply remembering to move the weights up the work as you

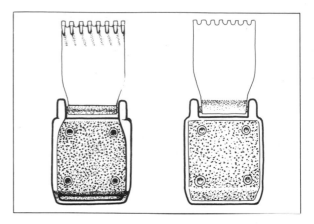

Inserted into the knitted fabric, weights keep the stitches in the needles as you knit; move them up regularly, especially when shaping

progress. Problems at the edge of the knitting can disappear if the weights are hung towards the side of the work and the yarn break tension checked. When knitting the full width of the machine, especially with lightweight yarns, extra weights are a great help. Where machines are supplied with cast-on combs these can be utilised throughout the knitting as necessary. They are gently hooked into the work and the claw weights evenly distributed along the comb.

As you will see weighting the work is a very important part of successful machine knitting, and you will soon find it a great advantage to have perhaps two more weights to call on as necessary. These are an inexpensive and invaluable extra.

· Waste yarn ·

Single bed machines will not produce the cast-on edge or the rib you associate with hand knitting, so you have to start the garment with some sort of hem. Unless you cast on by hand – as explained in Chapter 8 – you are going to use waste yarn, and in some machines in combination with a gadget called a cast-on comb, and a nylon cord specially supplied with your machine.

Waste yarn is knitted for six to ten rows before starting with the main yarn to be used for the garment, and serves to protect the first row of the main knitting from unravelling. In a sense it can be said to replace the cast-on of hand knitting. Casting on using waste yarn on a machine is known as 'open-edge' cast on. This indicates that the hem you are knitting has to be secured somehow to give a firm edge to the garment. You can also knit in the nylon cord for one row after the waste yarn before knitting the main yarn, thus separating the two and making it much easier to see the stitches when it comes to turning up the hem.

Apart from facilitating casting on, waste yarn can also be used to retain stitches which will be picked up at a later stage in the knitting, for example at neck and shoulder

Open-edge cast on using waste yarn. The nylon cord separates the waste yarn from the hem. The bottom of the first loose row is picked up, the nylon cord pulled out. The waste yarn drops away

edges, and sometimes when dividing the work for a 'v' neck. Used in this way it is the knitting machine's answer to the function of a stitch holder used in hand knitting.

So now you see why it is called waste yarn; it is pulled out and discarded when the technique it was part of is finished. It can be recycled, but it is easier to buy something cheap and disposable specially for the purpose. Your supplier generally has an oddment box of assorted cones of yarn. A word of warning –

don't use strong colours as a dark waste yarn will often shed fibres which will remain, permanently discolouring your knitting after the waste yarn has been stripped off.

· The nylon cord ·

There is a length of nylon cord supplied with most machines. It can be used to anchor the stitches after the first row of waste yarn has been knitted, and is gently removed once you have done enough knitting to hang the weights onto the work – about six rows. Then it can be used again to separate the waste yarn from the main yarn at the start of the hem. It enables you to see the first row of stitches more clearly when it comes to turning up the hem. Your instruction book will show you how to do this. However it is not absolutely necessary, and many beginners find it awkward to feed into the machine by hand. It isn't actually difficult, but apprehension makes it so! Start with the carriage at the left side of the work and feed in the cord, leaving a little tail about 25cm/10in below the feeder. After you have finished turning up the hem, the waste yarn can be removed by pulling out the nylon cord from the right. You will notice that the first stitch on the left has formed in such a way that the harder you pull, the tighter it makes a knot, and the cord will not pull out at all. So before pulling, undo this first stitch with an eyelet tool or a bodkin; it will then pull out easily.

The nylon cord can also be used where it is not possible to use holding position. When dividing for a 'v' neck, whether plain, stitch pattern or Fair Isle, it is usual to bring the stitches to left of centre out to holding position and finish the right side of the work first with the carriage set to hold, then return to the waiting stitches for the left side. However this method does not work when you are using the lace carriage, which is not designed to move over needles at holding position. In this case you can take the nylon cord and hand knit each stitch, keeping the cord loose and taking each needle right back to non-working position. You can now safely use both the lace and the knitting carriage over these long stitches with-

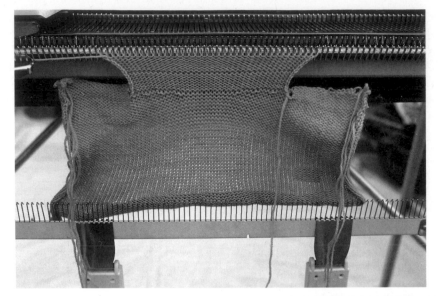

The shoulders are left on waste yarn whilst a finishing hem is knitted at the neckline. When this is turned up and cast off and the matching garment section knitted, the shoulders are joined on the machine, and the waste yarn stripped off

The left side of a 'v' neck is put onto waste yarn whilst the right side is finished, a useful method of retaining these stitches if the 'purl' side of the work is the right side, avoiding fluffing the work with the brushes if the stitches are retained at holding position

The needles at the left of a 'v' neck are knitted back to non-working position by hand using the nylon cord whilst finishing the right side. Useful when knitting lace designs where holding position is not possible

out them knitting and finish the right hand side of the work. Don't weight the knitting below the stitches not being worked, or one or two needles may be pulled back into working position and will decide to knit.

When you have finished the right side, you return to the stitches waiting at non-working position. Gently and carefully pull the nylon cord, holding the work and easing the stitches off the cord and onto the needles. This sounds a formidable task. Be assured it is not — it is only the written word that tends to make it seem so. Watch someone do it. After you have tried it a couple of times it will come easily.

· How to use the hand tools ·

The pushers A single bed machine is supplied with small plastic 'combs' called pushers. One of these has a plain edge which can be used to bring needles into working position across the bed of the machine. The opposite edge of this pusher is generally indented evenly, and is known as the 1×1 pusher, since it will select every other needle when it is placed behind the butts of needles in non-working position and drawn forward along the needle slots in the bed of the machine. You will probably have another pusher indented on both edges for 2×1 and 2×2 selection.

The transfer or eyelet tools These are double-ended tools of which there are generally three in your tool box; a 2×1, a 2×3, and a 3×1. The figures indicate the number of eyelets at each end. They are used for decreasing, and for picking up stitches from one part of the garment, eg a hem or a sleeve edge, and transferring them onto the needles. The single end is also used for casting off.

When decreasing, or transferring a stitch from one needle to the next, the eyelet tool is inserted into the hook of the needle, which you then pull forward so that the stitch goes behind the latch. Then, pushing the needle back to working position with a light but firm downward pressure of the tool, the stitch will ride over and close the latch, transferring itself onto the tool. It is then a simple matter to

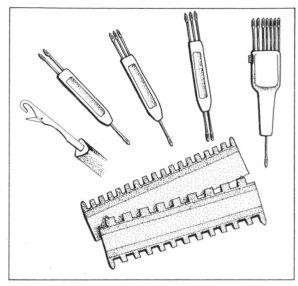

Learn to use the three-ended transfer tool to pick up hems with speed. The adjustable 7×1 tool makes fully-fashioned shaping easy. Casting off is quicker with the latch tool; needles easily selected with pushers

hook the tool onto the next needle, and ease the stitch off and into the needle hook with a gentle upward movement of the hand.

Knitters become very dextrous at this, which is why there are more than single eyelet tools. Decreasing and picking up stitches can become a very speedy process and you soon learn to move two or three stitches at once. When you become really confident it is probably worth buying the adjustable 7×1 transfer tool. A little screw at the side allows you to select and decrease up to the seventh stitch in from the edge of your work, or to make two or three decreases next to each other for fully-fashioned shaping.

Casting off with the eyelet tool The single eyelet tool can be used for casting off during knitting, for example at armhole edges and also for the final cast off, but it is not as swift a technique as the latch tool method.

With the carriage and yarn at the left of the machine, transfer the last stitch on the left to the needle to its right, and as you do so pull this needle out so that both stitches go behind the latch. Remove the eyelet tool and take the yarn over the hook. Hold it down as you draw the needle back, doing this by holding the butt of the needle. The yarn is drawn through both stitches, which can now be termed 'cast off'. Now transfer the new stitch to the next needle on the right and repeat the process, drawing the yarn end completely through the final stitch to secure the cast-off edge. Pull the needles right out to holding position as you do this.

If you are left handed you will probably find this technique easier to work starting from the right, with the carriage and yarn at the left.

The latch tool Mainly used for casting off and for picking up dropped stitches, this is simply a machine needle set into a plastic handle. Once the rhythm is mastered it is a speedy method for casting off at shoulders and necklines, and when joining sections of knitting.

Casting off with the latch tool If you are right handed you will find it easiest to knit your final row from left to right, thus ending with carriage and yarn at the right of the machine. You then begin to cast off from the left, inserting the hook of the latch tool into the first stitch and lifting it off the needle. It now rests in the hook of the latch tool. Slipping it behind the latch of the tool, and holding the latch down with your forefinger, the hook is inserted into the next stitch which is lifted off the needle. You now have two stitches on the latch tool; one in front of the latch and one behind. With a gentle pulling motion, allow the stitch behind the latch to slide forward. It closes the latch as it does so, comes off the needle, and is thus cast off. You slide the stitch now in the hook of the tool behind the latch, controlling the latch with your forefinger again, hook off the next stitch to the right and pull it through, and so on to the end, when you break the yarn and pull it right through the last stitch.

These techniques may appear painstaking and tedious at first, but gradually you will develop a regular rhythm and a satisfying speed. If you are left handed, of course, you will probably prefer to work in the opposite direction.

· Unravelling or unpicking work whilst on the machine ·

Unravelling is nothing to dread – you are bound to have to do this frequently for one reason or another, and it's not only the province of the beginner, experienced knitters are always doing it too! You will find it very easy and quick once you get the feel for it – you do not need to remove the work from the machine, simply hold the yarn and gently pull with a slightly upward and sideways movement. The stitch in the needle pulls tight and lifts the stitch of the previous row onto the needle as it comes undone. You may be surprised to see that several stitches will do this simultaneously. Soon you'll become so adept at the technique that you can pull back a complete row in a couple of swift movements.

· Yarn for beginners ·

Those of us who tend to hoard things generally have bags and boxes stuffed with scraps of material and left over balls of wool and the first inclination is to rummage around collecting oddments of knitting wool to practise with on the new machine. Although it is nearly always possible to use hand knitting yarns on the machine, when you are learning you will find it much easier if you buy a couple of cones of acrylic yarn in contrasting colours. This is cheap, runs through the machine smoothly, and is the perfect yarn for practice. Choose light, bright colours which are easy on the eyes. Black, dark brown, navy and bottle green should be banned from your practice sessions. The light coloured yarn allows you to see your stitches easily as you knit and when you use the tools for hand techniques – decreasing and casting off for example. Your hand knitting yarn can be used up when you are more proficient.

· How long will it take to learn? ·

This depends on so many things. You simply must not be pressured, but work methodically through your instruction book, mastering each technique as you go. Have patience! You will soon find you are doing things with ease.

4
TENSION

TENSION is expressed as the number of stitches and rows to a 10cm/4in square. From this the requirements for a measured garment can be calculated. Your instruction book may have a section on tension in relation to yarn thickness and to stitch patterns, but what it may not tell you is how to relate stitch tension to garment size.

The most important piece of information, the foundation of your success as a machine knitter, is the information on your pattern concerning tension. It may well be the one item you are inclined to ignore, especially if as a hand knitter you were able to knit successfully without bothering to knit a test piece – it's a time consuming task when hand knitting. However when machine knitting a tension square is quickly made and vital to success, so it is unforgivable to omit it. At least when handknitting you have some idea of the finished garment width as you knit, and can measure length as you go, adding an inch or knitting less than the pattern states where necessary, though this is a less than ideal method of working. Not so with the machine, which distorts the knitting so that it does not reveal its true dimensions until it has been off the needles for some time and the stitches have settled. You certainly can't measure the width and length of the work you are knitting whilst it is on the machine. Once off, the piece of knitting will lengthen as the work relaxes, and thereby lose width, so there has to be a standard method of measurement which everyone who is concerned with machine knitting agrees upon. This is called a tension square. After giving the material requirements the tension information in given patterns usually reads something like this:

Tension: 30sts and 40rs to 10cm/4in, tension dial at approximately 6

Why approximately? It's not that the pattern writer is showing indecision, it's that allowance is being given for variation of tension between machines. No two machines, even of the same make and model, will necessarily give the same number of rows and stitches to the centimetre/inch from the same ball of yarn at the same tension. The eager new knitter, therefore, will fiddle about trying to achieve the stitch count given by knitting various squares using tensions from 5 to 7, if at tension 6 the square does not measure 30sts × 40rs. Very often the stitches are correct, but the rows are not, or vice versa, and it looks as though the tension is impossible to achieve.

Most knitters have problems at this point, and cry out in desperation: 'I've bought the right yarn and tried everything, but I can't get the tension right, what do I do?' The secret is not to worry about achieving the exact row and stitch count indicated by the pattern, but to concentrate on finding the tension which best suits the yarn and stitch pattern. Your tension square should handle sympathetically for its purpose – soft and pliable but not too slack for a sweater, maybe a little firmer for a jacket. Perhaps the tension the pattern suggested is right for the yarn even though you cannot achieve the stated number of rows and stitches, in which case you should stick to the suggested tension setting and adapt the pattern accordingly.

As soon as you have learned to do this you are free to use any yarn you choose, providing it is suitable for the garment you want to make. This suddenly brings within your grasp all the industrial yarns that lie temptingly and in-expensively on the shelves. So *you* decide how many stitches to cast on and how many rows to knit, and from the pattern you take the design – the shape, the stitch and the details.

· Knitting a tension square ·

Set RC to 000
Cast on 60sts in main yarn and the chosen tension
K 20rs MY
K 2rs contrast yarn
K 30rs MY
Pull out the 21st N to L and R of 0, and hand knit the stitch with a length of contrast yarn
K 30rs MY
K 2rs contrast yarn
K 20rs MY
Remove the work from the machine by taking the yarn out of the yarn feeder, breaking it off, and running the carriage over the 60sts. The work will be released from the machine.

· Recording your tension ·

Whatever stitch pattern you are using, the instructions for the tension square are the same. If you wish to try various tensions on the same piece, divide them with twenty rows of main knitting between the contrast yarn. It's no use thinking you will remember what tension you have used on each piece, so do label them somehow. If there is no need to wash the samples before measuring, then use a little swing ticket, the sort used by shops for garment prices, and available from stationers to mark each section, writing in the necessary tension details on it.

If you are using yarn that has been spun in oil the tension squares need to be washed in order to give a true measurement. Ordinary washing up liquid will do, then rinse and squeeze in a towel to get rid of excess water before drying. It follows that you can't label these in the same way. However, machine knitters will always find a solution to a problem, and many prefer the following methods for all their squares, since swing tickets have an irritating habit of intertwining

amongst themselves when several tension squares are kept together.

Imagine you are knitting a square using tension 6· – you want to record this on the knitting, so stop at row 14 of the first 20 rows, with carriage at the right. Using the single end of an eyelet tool, transfer the fifth stitch from the right onto the sixth needle, leaving the empty needle in working position. Now transfer the seventh stitch onto the eighth needle and so on until you have made six transfers. Now miss two stitches, and make a further transfer making sure that all empty needles are left in working position. Carry on knitting up to row 20. In this way you can very effectively knit all your information into the square. If you always do this at the same place you will soon be able to recognise the tension of a sample at a glance and no confusion can arise when you indicate tensions below T2··.

Another method of recording this infor-mation is to use a contrast colour. Knit to row 14 as before then, taking a length of contrast yarn, hand knit the fifth to tenth stitches from the right. Miss two stitches, and knit the 13th and 14th stitches in contrast. Carry on with the knitting as before.

Both these methods work very well for stocking stitch samples. When knitting lace patterns it is best to use contrast yarn on a knit row of the pattern to avoid confusion. You will find it better to use the transfer method when knitting a Fair Isle pattern. If there is an instance when the stitch pattern makes neither method suitable, then put in your information as you knit the first contrast rows. You may find it better to knit four contrast rows here, entering your details onto your work at row three by which ever method you prefer. Again remember to be consistent, whichever side of the knitting is used for the right side of your garment, if you always read the tension information on the smooth side it will always be on the left.

There is a very good reason for the tension swatches to be this rather extravagant size. As the edges of knitting tend to distort, a true reading of rows and stitches to centimetres or

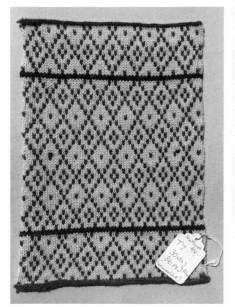

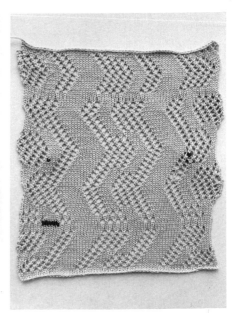

inches is best taken in the middle of a piece of work. If you are short of yarn you will have to resort to recycling your samples, but remember to record all the information in your notebook – yarn, tension, rows and stitches to a 10cm/4in square. You can be sure that if you forget to do this you are bound to need the information!

· Relaxing ·

Because the machine distorts the knitting you cannot expect to remove a sample from your machine, measure it, work out your pattern and immediately knit a garment to a given size. A glance at any of the illustrations in this book which show the structure of knitted fabric can help you to understand the structure of the stitch and how the horizontal pull of the knitted fabric on the machine will contract once it has been removed, altering the width and the length. After the initial removal, the stitches will continue to settle over quite a long period of time. This is known as allowing the knitting to relax, a very apt and descriptive term for the behaviour of yarn after the stress it has under-gone on the machine.

It is best to leave the samples overnight. Though yarns behave differently, and many knitters cheat a bit, experience has taught that three or four hours ought to be the minimum relaxation period. It's a good idea to work

(*left*) The tension for this Fair Isle sample recorded on a swing ticket; (*centre*) here the tension has been coded in by transferring the stitches making it easy to see – tension 6· was used; (*right*) on this lace tension square 4 rows of main colour were knitted instead of two contrast rows, and contrast yarn was used to enter tension information, indicating tension 5

samples in the evening, so that you can make a start the next day. Or, if it doesn't seem too antisocial, before the family is up and about in the morning, to be ready later in the day.

· Preparation and measurement ·

Swatches from wool spun in oil will need to be washed, and this can be done as soon as they come off the machine. The knitting will fill out considerably after washing so the tension chosen should appear fairly loose. Experience will show the tension to use. The difference between a stringy unwashed sample of angora, for example, and its delicate fluffy feel after washing is like the difference between chalk and cheese.

All tension squares need to be pressed according to the spinner's instructions. If there are none, details for the treatment of various yarns will be found in Appendix 1. Pin your square to the ironing board without distorting it and try not to push the little piece of knitting about with the iron – 'press' means exactly what it says.

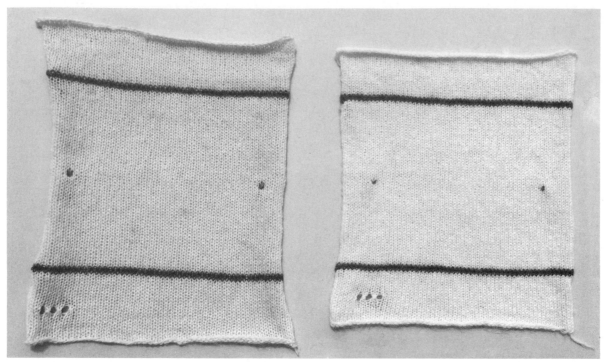

Here are two identical tension squares knitted in industrial angora 'in oil'; the square on the right has been washed and pressed. The unwashed sample gives 32 stitches and 54 rows to a 10cm/4in square; when washed, the measurements are 36 stitches and 56 rows

There are three ways of taking measurements from this square. The simplest is to place a ruler – much firmer and more accurate than a tape measure – horizontally between the marker stitches, and count the number of stitches to 10cm/4in. Then place it vertically on the back of the sample, in the middle of the square, and count the number of rows to 10cm/4in.

There is a useful little object called a green rule, which many knitters find more accurate and which is used between the contrast yarn markers to measure the number of stitches, and the contrast rows, measuring in the centre of the swatch. The green rule will give a reading from 27rs and 18sts up to 100rs and 80sts, relating to a 10cm/4in square of work. It was originally designed for use with the Knitmaster charting device, the Knitradar, but has since proved an inexpensive and reliable method of tension measurement for knitters on all machines.

The charting device, which comes separately or is built in to some machines, uses this standard tension square, in combination with a centimetre rule provided, or the green rule. The Passap and Pfaff machines recommend that the numbers of stitches and rows are calculated from the chart they supply, given the measurements of a test square of 100rs × 100sts. However their charting device is based on the 10cm/4in measurement. Remember that if you are planning a garment combining different stitch patterns, you will have to work tension squares for each one.

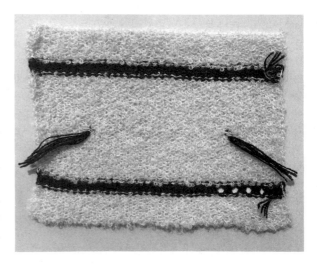

The tension for this square, knitted on the chunky machine, has been coded into the contrast rows

· The tension square for chunky machines ·

The principle of this tension square is the same as the one for the standard machines but, as you might imagine, there are half the number of stitches and rows between the markers.

RC 000
Cast on 40sts MY in chosen tension
K 10rs MY
K 2rs contrast yarn
K 15rs MY
Pull out the 11th Ns to L and R of 0, and hand knit them with lengths of contrast yarn – leave long enough 'tails' of yarn to hold on to as you knit the next row, this ensures that the stitches will knit.
K 15rs MY
K 2rs contrast yarn
K 10rs MY

The swatch is obviously prepared for measurement in the same way as the standard square, and is measured in the same way. If you are knitting on every other needle on a standard gauge machine then knit this size square.

Some machines have separate intarsia carriages. When working intarsia designs you must knit the tension square with the intarsia carriage rather than hope that your main carriage will give the same result on the same stitch setting. It is possible that you will knit part of a garment with the main carriage and part with the intarsia carriage. You will need to balance them to achieve a consistent tension. Every time you do this make thorough notes of yarn, stitch settings and resultant tension. It may be that you will observe a relationship between the tension settings of both carriages, and will be able to adjust accordingly once this is established. If you are very lucky the tensions may be balanced and no adjustment will be necessary.

· Estimating yarn quantities ·

There is no difficulty in estimating yarn quantities when using industrial yarns purchased from your local machine knitting shop. You stagger out of the door with several huge cones which have been weighed and paid for. After you have used as much as you need, you return the unwanted yarn. As long as there is a useful quantity remaining, this will be weighed, and you will either be given a credit note or a refund.

It is important to record all the details of garment size, yarn specifications and quantity used, against the day when you see something similar and need to decide whether there is sufficient yarn for your purpose. If you are using only one yarn throughout the knitting you only need to weigh the garment – before it is washed if the yarn is in oil – and record pattern size and quantity used. If you have mixed ends, then weigh each cone before you start, and again when you have finished, do your sums and record the results in your notebook.

When it comes to buying cones of given weights and there is no indication of required quantities on the wrapper or, if through mail order, in the catalogue, life can become more difficult. Finding patterns in your chosen yarn and similar to the design you want to knit can help. An allowance of a little extra is wise, and many mail order firms supply both cones and 50 or 100gm balls of their yarns which can make up your requirements. It is an expensive sweater that needs 550gm of yarn that only comes in 250gm cones.

Buying locally where you can is obviously more economical when you have a good relationship with your supplier. He will usually keep a cone of the same dye lot for a few days until you need it. If you can knit an exact half of your work – say the back and a sleeve of a sweater – put this on your scales and multiply the weight by two. You can hardly go wrong, but it is wise to allow a few grammes extra for the neck finish and emergencies.

Make it a rule to weigh in before you start a garment and weigh again when it is finished. Record all the information, it will be invaluable for future reference.

5
TECHNIQUES

ALL the basic knitting techniques are explained in your instruction book, but due to limited space these are only the bare essentials. There is enough information to get you going certainly, but you are left to learn quite a lot by trial and error, which can use up precious hours of time.

Everyone reacts differently to their first hours on a knitting machine. An ability, understanding, and lack of fear of mechanical objects, manual dexterity and a knowledge of stitch construction give some knitters a head start, and make them the envy of those who eye the machine with great suspicion and whose fingers behave like sausages when manipulating the tools. Just as some people always produced untidy ink-spattered work in their school days while others handed in work which was always clean and beautifully presented, so there are knitters who can never find the right tools, whose nylon cord has more knots than the machine has needles and whose tiny piece of knitting hangs forlornly on the machine looking as though it has been used to clean a frying pan. If you are one of these, take heart, quite often it is the impatient, scruffy knitter who in the end shows the greatest imagination and creativity. Once you have understood and tamed your machine it will become a willing servant to your ideas.

Few other items of equipment have more bits and pieces ready to get lost, catch in your clothes and hair or fall continually to the floor than the knitting machine. It runs away with many people at first, and those without patience certainly acquire this virtue while learning to machine knit. Those who tend to live in happy disarray have to learn to bring a little order into their lives, at least in the area around the knitting machine. Simply developing habits such as always putting everything back in the same place is a good beginning. When the telephone rings, don't take your latch tool with you when you go to answer it, it may end up in the bathroom, and when the hunt is on for the missing item you completely forget that you slipped in there before you returned to the machine! Good knitting habits will make the whole knitting process smoother and easier for you, and working methodically will help you to understand the function of the machine so much more quickly, so that when the knitting falls to the floor you won't be asking 'why did it do that?' but 'what did I do wrong?' On the whole the machine is always right, and reminds you of this frequently with silent reproach. It is up to you to develop a sensitivity towards it, and you can help yourself to do this by being organised in your approach. Whenever you start to knit, develop the habit of checking through your machine set up, from front to back. The sequence listed below is one logical checking system. However if you feel better starting from the back and working to the front it doesn't matter, as long as you have a system that works for you.

1 Yarn(s) in the feeder(s) and feeder gate closed
2 Pattern buttons or levers selected where necessary
3 Check whether carriage is set to hold or normal as required
4 Tension dial set to requirements
5 Change knob or side levers in the required position
6 Pattern card checked and lock lever set, if used

7 Row counter set or reset as necessary, tripper set

8 Charting device checked and tripper set if being used

9 Yarn running correctly and smoothly through the tension mast

10 After pattern selection row, remember to release lock lever of pattern if used

It looks a laborious task when written down, but checking through systematically in whichever way suits you best soon becomes second nature and the whole performance is accomplished by a quick but thorough glance.

· Why things go wrong when knitting ·

In spite of all your care and discipline things do occasionally go wrong. It may be a comfort to know that the more you knit, the less you make mistakes, and when they are made, they are easier to put right.

Problems often arise when you return to the machine to carry on knitting after a break. In that period of time, however short, evil spirits, gremlins, call them what you will, seem to get to work and as soon as you move the carriage you are in trouble. The most usual cause has nothing to do with hobgoblins or the jinx you may imagine lurks in your machine but simply arises from the fact that when the knitting action is not continuous, the yarn from the tension mast gradually slackens as the take-up spring relaxes. When you start to knit again, the yarn, which has also slackened beneath the carriage, either becomes wrapped around the brushes and the carriage jams or it forms a huge loop at the beginning of the row which then gets caught in the brushes so that the carriage jams in the middle of the row. Your instruction book will show you how to remove the sinker plate assembly, and how to remove the carriage from the machine without the stitches coming off the needles, though if you are lucky you may be able to disentangle the yarn without removing any part of the carriage. By far the best course is to try to prevent it from happening at all. When you return to your machine, run one hand beneath the carriage to make sure any loop that has formed between the edges of the knitting and the yarn feed is free of the brushes, and with the other hand pull the slack yarn up from the feeder at the same time. At the back of the machine pull the slack yarn downwards from the yarn guide towards the cone. Then with a final check beneath the carriage, carry on knitting.

The carriage will also jam if the yarn flow is impeded in some way. So if you come to a sharp halt in the middle of the row and the yarn is not wound around the brushes you may find that a knot is the culprit. If it has travelled as far as the knitting, and won't go through the needle, then you will have to take the carriage off and unravel the row to the beginning, making corrections in the row counter and pattern as necessary. Then pull the yarn with the knot in it well down below the carriage, at the side, and hold it there as you knit the row again. Take care that the loop formed does not catch in the brushes over the next two or three rows giving rise to further problems.

A knot can also cause trouble at any point through the tension mast, pulling the stitches tight in the needles. The yarn will sometimes slacken under the carriage during knitting if the carriage is taken too far beyond the edge of the work, or if the knitting action is uneven and jerky. It is better to unpick any rows affected by tight knitting, or the finished work will be uneven and spoiled. Take care whenever you stop to perform any manual technique – increasing, decreasing, turning up a hem etc, it always pays to check everything over before starting to knit again if the handwork has taken you a few minutes.

If you have constant looping or dropped stitches at the end of rows it is nearly always only necessary to adjust the tension of the yarn in the tension assembly to eradicate this. Check the tension by pulling the yarn end down. If the take-up spring is immediately released then the tension in the assembly is too loose. If the spring is not released at all, or only very slowly, it is too tight.

So when things go wrong, as they do for

even the most experienced knitters, a routine check of carriage and yarn will help to discover the cause. Initial checking takes less than thirty seconds and is well worth it, but if things still go wrong, as they do occasionally however careful you think you have been, the same care in fault finding will pay dividends. It really is invaluable to watch an experienced knitter in full swing, to see how methodically the knitting action is performed, how faults are dealt with and how problems are forseen and therefore often avoided.

If you are fortunate to discover a good machine knitting class, you will find the tutor will talk through everything demonstrated and explain every move made, welcoming questions and being willing to show you the same technique several times. Don't be shy of asking questions and don't imagine they are silly. Tutors are always glad of them because they often illuminate a point that has been overlooked.

One of the first things you notice about a machine knitter in action is the constant manipulation of the claw weights. They are always being moved for one reason or another. The experienced knitter is automatically sensitive to the weighting requirements of the knitting. Notice too that the carriage is pushed and pulled along the bed from the side of the handle, and not pressed down onto the bed. The movement is light, and the knitter's hand is sensitive to the response of the machine. The carriage must never be forced. If it feels as though it will not knit, don't be tempted to bully it; there is sure to be a solution which does not involve breaking the needles and risking damage to the bed.

If you do damage a needle don't rush to change it – you may be able to straighten it or a bent latch with little effort. However if the latch still remains 'sticky' you will need to replace the needle. Don't panic, needles are very easy to change; it is simply a matter of pushing out the retainer bar, exchanging needles and pushing the bar back into place. Your instruction book will give you detailed instructions, and the process can be performed

with knitting on the machine. Be sure to throw the damaged needle away – nothing is more annoying than going to the trouble of replacing a needle, only to find that the replacement is also damaged. You may be tempted to see if you can make do with a damaged needle – don't. Although it might be able to cope with stocking stitch it will probably fail to tuck efficiently and rogue needles almost always show up when they are selected for patterning.

· Automatic techniques ·

As soon as they have set up a new machine and actually made it knit, the natural progression for the impatient beginner is to try the automatic patterning, particularly the two colour or Fair Isle technique. It certainly is very exciting to put a chosen card into a slot, set the appropriate levers or buttons, and churn out a strip of Fair Isle; to watch how the machine selects the needles for tucking patterns, how surface texture is achieved with both slip and tuck stitch, and how the second colour is 'laid in' in the weaving technique. The adverts often say how clever these machines are, and that is probably the first adjective that will spring to your lips as you discover what the machine can do.

The instruction book will illustrate the automatic techniques which your machine is capable of. These are achieved either by punchcard or electronically.

Two colour or Fair Isle work Two colour refers to the number of colours possible in one row. More colours are possible by using the slip stitch technique. Always work Fair Isle one whole tension number larger than stocking stitch for the same yarn. Avoid large floats or strands at the back of the work on patterns for small children. These occur on large repeat patterns and catch in fingers when garments are put on. Children look better in small detail patterns in any case.

On older machines, bring out the first needle of every row to holding position with the carriage set for normal knitting. The needle knits back in the second colour, keeping the edges of the work neat. On contemporary machines this is done automatically.

When planning colour schemes it helps to wrap your chosen colours around a piece of card in order to gauge the effect. The same technique can be used when planning stripes. Play with the pattern. Lock the card, change the colours both in the main feeder and feeder 2. Your instruction book will show you several ways to vary the same pattern, and you will probably think of some interesting new ways of your own.

Slip stitch Slip, skip, part, empty and free move are all different terms for the same function on different machines. When the carriage is on this setting, *but not set to read the pattern card*, it can be moved across the work without knitting. However any needles at hold will knit back and, unless there is yarn in the feeder, will drop their stitches. Combined with the pattern card, slip technique produces a subtle relief pattern and if the purl side is used as the right side, the slipped stitches give an embossed effect. Multi-coloured slip patterns produce a Fair Isle effect on the smooth side of the knitting, but care has to be taken to adjust the tension so that the knitted fabric remains soft and pliable because this technique produces a thicker fabric than normal knitting. You will find the tension square measures very differently from one in stocking stitch and you will need more rows and more stitches to achieve a similar area on the same tension.

Tuck stitch Endless pattern variations can be achieved by manipulating colour, stitch pattern, tension and yarn thickness when using this technique. When compared to a stocking stitch sample in the same yarn, tuck stitch needs less stitches but more rows to achieve a similar area. When the card with alternate holes punched throughout is used, a cellular fabric is produced, very useful for producing warm cotton garments for people who are allergic to wool. A tension one whole number less than that for stocking stitch in the same yarn is advisable for some patterns.

Weaving This produces a more sophisticated fabric, suitable for more formal garments. Because the woven yarn is caught into the supporting stitch and not knitted, it thus has less length. The fabric does not have the elasticity usually associated with the knitted stitch. Use a comparatively fine yarn as a backing, and try textured, fancy yarns in the weaving arm to achieve some interesting effects. Don't forget to set the brushes, or the weaving yarn will not catch into the main knitting.

Lace Most modern machines give the facility to create lacy patterns. If you have ever knitted lacy garments by hand you will appreciate that the machine equivalent of knitting two stitches together, wool over the needle, or knit one, slip one, pass slip stitch over, could be quite a complex affair. It's not in fact all that complex, but it does differ from other automatic patterning, and so merits some explanation.

In machine terms the solution is to provide a separate lace carriage. The sole function of this carriage is to transfer stitches from one needle to another where selected – knitting two together in hand knitting terms. After all the necessary transfer actions are completed, then the knitting carriage, waiting patiently at the right of the machine, knits two rows. The transfer carriage *only* rotates the pattern card, it does not activate the tripper of the row counter or the charting device. It is only when the knit carriage is used that the knitting grows, and rows are registered. The knitting carriage does not rotate the pattern card, because there is no patterning on these rows. The lace cards have directional arrows for the movement of the transfer carriage, and a 'U' turn arrow for the two knit carriage rows. The more lace carriage rows there are, the more complex the pattern. It all sounds very complicated, but you soon get into the swing of using both carriages, and the work grows quickly. Mistakes are simple to put right since, after transferring stitches back to their own needles you have arrived at the return knit rows, so it is easy to reset the card. The same tension square is used as for all patterns, the contrast rows being worked on the knit rows on the pattern card. The lace carriage differs from one machine to another. The table at the end of Chapter 2 explains this.

The lace carriage will not pass over needles in holding position. Alternative methods for retaining stitches whilst completing other sections of knitting have to be used when dividing for the neck and for neckline shaping.

Knitmaster also have a facility called punch lace available. Some very attractive effects can be achieved with this technique, which entails using a fine 2/30 cotton – known as 30's cotton, and very like sewing cotton – in feeder two. When patterning, the main yarn and the cotton knit together in unpunched areas, the cotton knits on its own where the pattern is punched. Some people use a transparent nylon filament to produce the lace look, but this produces a rather stiff fabric. You may prefer to use cotton a shade darker than the main yarn, or a contrast darker tone. When the main yarn is itself a 3 or 4 ply equivalent cotton, the fabric knitted has a heavy, attractive, silky feel to it, which is very nice for smart summer clothes.

Plating Some machines are supplied with a small alternative yarn feeder which enables plating technique to be worked. This is a knitting technique which uses two yarns: a firm backing yarn and a lightweight plating yarn. The yarns are threaded into the special feeder in such a way that as they knit the main yarn shows on the knit side, the plating yarn on the purl side. Tuck stitch patterns look particularly good when plated, the design showing up with a delicate shadowy effect.

Plating has its origins in industry where a fine expensive yarn could be used more economically if backed by a cheaper and thicker yarn. You will find that the combination of Shetland as a backing yarn with a fine cashmere in the plating feed works very well for example, and cotton combined with wool in this way can provide warmth without the irritating tickle.

Single motif The single motif is a development of the Fair Isle technique whereby part of a punchcard design or a punchcard with a single design on it can be isolated and knitted at a selected position on a garment. Your instruction book illustrates how to set up your machine for this, and how to weave separate strands of main yarn up either side of the motif as you knit. This is an important detail of this technique since it eliminates gaps which would otherwise occur between the design and the rest of the knitting. It is possible to extend the width of your design beyond the width of the punchcard to a certain extent by hand selecting the extra needles. By knitting a garment sideways you can use the width of the card as the height of the design. The width of the design on the garment then runs the length of the punchcard, and since you can join punchcards this is not restricted. This is particularly useful when you want to knit-in someone's name where the 24 stitch limitation of the punchcard or the 60 stitches of the electronic sheet would not provide sufficient width. Don't confuse this technique with intarsia!

· Manual technique ·

Intarsia Intarsia means inlay, and refers to blocks of colour 'laid in' to a background. In the Fair Isle technique, stitch pattern is governed and restricted by selected needles in relation to a pattern card. Intarsia is a non-automatic colour technique worked in most cases by a separate carriage which brings out all the needles to upper working position with the latches open. Yarns are then laid over the needles by hand according to the design, and the intarsia carriage moved over them. As the stitches are knitted the needles are brought out ready for the next row.

To start with, it's best to keep your design simple, though of course you can have as many colour changes as you like in a row. The chosen design can be drawn onto a charting device, but if you don't have one you can draw the garment shape, full size, on ratio graph paper and work out the stitches and rows for the shapes from your tension square.

Although this is obviously slower than automatic patterning, the reward lies in the freedom of design. If you enjoy knitting pictures or large abstract patterns you will want the facility for intarsia, either built into the machine or as a separate carriage. Another advantage is the lack of floats or strands of yarn at the back of the work, the yarns being neatly woven around each other as you change them.

· Starting patterning ·

You are nearly sure to knit your first practice pattern piece until something goes wrong. Taken off the machine – perhaps by accident rather than design – the scrap of knitting is treated with reverence and wonder!

How the machine selects for patterning varies from one manufacturer to another. It need not worry you, as it is not necessary to understand the mechanics entirely, but it is important to understand how the pattern card relates to the knitting machine. You have to understand that the machine cannot 'know' what to do. It can only respond to your instructions via the selected buttons and levers, which motivate cams in the carriage to direct needles for the type of pattern selected. Which needles will be chosen is decided by the pattern card. The information on this is the punched holes on the card, or in the case of electronic machines, the black squares on the sheet. Each row of the pattern card is 'read' by levers or pins, and transmitted to the needles in working position at the back of the carriage or in the needlebed.

· How the machine reads the pattern ·

Your instruction book will tell you how to knit in pattern, but probably not what happens as you knit the pattern. It is important to realise that the information for each pattern row must be in the machine one row ahead all the time. If you think about it, this is logical because on your last row of plain knitting you select the needles to pattern on the next row. Then before you start the first pattern row you set the carriage to slip, tuck, Fair Isle, weave or whatever pattern you choose. You then knit the first pattern row. As you do so, the card turns up to the next row, and the information for that row is conveyed to the pattern mechanism. So you have knitted row 1, and the card reads row 2, the pattern row which you will now knit. It may be easier to understand if you say that the machine is ready to knit row 2. As you knit row 2, in goes row 3 information, and so on. The card number is always one row ahead of the row number. Have a few 'dummy runs', with the card in the card slot and no knitting on the machine until you feel you understand the process.

Have a close look at a pattern card. You will realise immediately that the row of punched holes in line with the number 1 at the right could not possibly be the row 1 that you knit. This figure represents the first row on the card when it is turned down inside the card slot being 'read' by the card reading mechanism. On Knitmaster cards it is the fifth row below the figure, on Jones and Toyota machines it is the seventh row and it is the fourth on Singer machines. If, for example, you were using a Knitmaster card in a Jones machine, you would have to lock it on row 3 in order to pick up the first row of the pattern.

If a piece of work should fall off the machine while you are working in pattern, there are one or two extra things you will have to take into consideration when replacing it on the needles or you could end up with a tell-tale line across the work.

Firstly you must ensure that you replace stitches onto the correct needles. If you should have 104 stitches, 52 to the left and 52 to the right of 0, it's no use having 54 on one side and 50 on the other, your needles will still pattern in the same place as before, so you will have a two stitch discrepancy.

If you try to pick up stitches from the last knitted row some of the stitches may run down the work as you pick up others. It is much easier to pick up stitches a couple of rows below the last row you knitted. You then pull out the rows above this, turning the pattern card and the row counter back at the end of each row pulled out. Then lock the card.

Check that all the stitches are in the needles and tidy up the yarn by pulling it down towards the cones at the back of the machine.

Whenever you need to unpick rows make a note of the number on the row counter and on the pattern card, lock the pattern card and deactivate the row counter tripper before you start. Sometimes a row does not knit, but the pattern card turns up. To correct this turn the card back one row first. Check whether the row counter had been tripped too. Remember it is consistently one number behind the card. If your row counter shows row 6, the pattern card will show row 7; as you knitted row 6, row 7 was selected.

· Resetting the pattern ·

You can preset the row locked on the pattern card without actually knitting. Set the Knitmaster carriage to slip, with side levers forward. It must pass the touch levers beneath the card slot to have that information transferred to the pattern drums at the back of the carriage. The Jones and Toyota have the carriage set to part or empty and to select the pattern, the preset row is slipped over, the needles are selected in the bed of the machine and come out ready to knit the row locked on the card. Resetting the pattern is generally done from left to right.

Once the information is in the pattern mechanism you are ready to set your machine to knit again. Remember to check your carriage settings from front to back, to reactivate the tripper of the row counter and to release the card. It is extremely irritating to make another mistake immediately after correcting one.

The need to reset the pattern most frequently occurs when shaping necklines, where the right side of the neck is finished first, and the left is then finished to match. There are three methods of holding the stitches at the left side, and whichever method is used, the pattern has to be reset before knitting this side to match the right, so it is well worth considering the techniques together. They are described below, using a 'v' neck as an example. Remember to replace both yarns in the correct feeders where necessary if you are working a Fair Isle pattern.

Using holding position Bring the needles to the left of centre 0 to holding position and set the carriage to hold. Make a note of row number and card number. Finish the right side, replacing the empty needles to non-working position.

Now replace the needles at holding position to working position with the eyelet tool so that the stitches are back in the hooks. You cannot preset a row with needles at holding position. Preset the row according to the patterning mechanism of your machine as described for resetting the pattern above. Your carriage must be set to slip over the replaced stitches whilst presetting the row, this time from right to left. Join in the main yarn, set carriage to pattern, reset row counter, unlock card and carry on knitting.

Using nylon cord In this method the stitches at the left are knitted manually with the nylon cord. Each one is pushed back to non-working position as it is worked. After finishing the right side, carefully replace the stitches on the nylon cord in the needles with the 'unpicking' movement, and preset the row accordingly. Replace the main yarn in the feeder, set carriage to pattern, reset row counter, unlock card and then knit the left side.

Using waste yarn The stitches at the left can be knitted onto waste yarn. Record the row number and the pattern card number and lock the card. Thread the feeder with waste yarn. Bring the stitches at the right to holding position. Set the carriage for normal knitting and to hold, and knit the stitches at the left with several rows of waste yarn. End with carriage at the left and break the yarn.

Move carriage to the right – the stitches on waste yarn drop off the needles. Replace these needles to non-working position. Replace the needles in holding position at the right to working position using the eyelet tool. Set the carriage to slip, *but not to pattern*. Move it to the left. Knitmaster carriages simply need to pass the touch levers below the pattern card slot completely to record the pattern, and the carriage can come back to the right. Machines which select the needles in the bed should now be set to read the card, and to part or empty.

Move the carriage over the stitches to the right, and the needles for patterning will come forward. Thread the main yarn into the feeder, set the carriage to pattern, reset the row counter and unlock the card. Finish knitting the right side, replacing the empty needles to non-working position.

Replace the stitches on waste yarn into the correct needles. Do not remove the waste yarn. Reset the pattern as already described. With carriage at the left join in the yarn, reset all relevant knobs and levers as before and finish knitting the left side. The waste yarn can now be removed.

Each of these methods has its value. If you are knitting light coloured yarn, the less holding position is used the better, because the needles can make the waiting stitches dirty. They are best on waste yarn or knitted back with the nylon cord. If the purl side of the work is to be the right side of the garment then the waiting stitches are better on waste yarn. The brushes on the carriage tend to fluff up the yarn under needles at hold if a considerable amount of knitting needs to be done. Some people simply stick a piece of Sellotape under the needles at holding position to protect the knitting. It's a simple and workable answer to the problem. It is not possible to use the lace carriage with needles at holding position so the work should be divided after the two knit rows, and the waiting section put onto waste yarn or the nylon cord.

A disadvantage of knitting the stitches back to non-working position with the nylon cord is that the weight of the work sometimes pulls an odd needle forward to working position, or needles are accidently knocked to this position. They of course knit and then have to be unpicked.

· Practising patterning ·
You may be so keen to make something patterned that this piece of advice may go unheeded, but if you can muster the patience, it is well worth practising these methods on small samples. If the first time you knit a 'v' neck on the front of a garment is also the first time you endeavour to use a pattern card, some prior practice will be especially import-ant. Here is a suitable practice piece:

Choose a pattern card suitable for the stitch pattern you wish to practise, put it into the card slot and lock it onto row 1.
Cast on 60sts WY and K several rs
The knitmaster machines will already have the pattern setting for the first row in the pattern drums, having been past the touch levers. End with carriage at the right of the bed. Machines which select the needles in the bed can be preset on the last row of the waste yarn, so knit this last row from left to right.
Put MY in the feeder, set carr for chosen pattern, set RC 000, release the card
K 40rs in pattern, ending with carr at R
Note row number and card number
Divide for the neck in whichever method you wish to practise, remembering to reset the row counter where necessary
Finish R side first
Decrease 1st at the neck edge on the first and every following third row 10 times in all.
K 2rs straight, RC 70
Put remaining 20sts onto WY
Finish L side to match, resetting the pattern as described previously

· What went wrong? ·
When machine knitting is all new and strange it's very easy to forget one important feature in a sequence, and to spend quite a few minutes totally baffled, unable to work out why the machine is not doing what you thought you had set it to do. The most common disaster is the knitting coming inexplicably off the needles and falling to the floor. What went wrong?
· You forgot to put the yarn in the feeder?

· You put yarn in the feeder, forgot to close the gate and it slipped out?

· You set the carriage to slip without yarn in the feeder; the needles were in hold but the carriage wasn't? Remember that if you have some needles in hold and some in working position your carriage must be set to both hold and slip.

· If the work knits in the second colour only in Fair Isle technique, then you are trying to knit needles back to working position from hold whilst patterning. Needles at holding position must be manually returned to working position when using the pattern cards.

· With some needles at hold and some at working position the carriage was set to slip. If all the needles knit you had forgotten to set the carriage to hold.

· On Knitmaster machines, if the pattern is 'lost' and inaccurate, then you have not taken the carriage completely past the touch levers, and if your machine does not pattern at all you have forgotten to put the side levers back. Remember, too, that it's no use expecting any machine to tuck or weave properly without its extra brushes being added to the sinker assembly or brought into place with the flick of a lever.

I can't emphasize enough how important it is to make notes. When disasters happen – and it's no good pretending they don't – nothing is more frustrating than to discover, having painstakingly replaced the work onto the machine, that you had forgotten to record the row and card number. This must be the first thing you do before beginning to rectify mistakes, particularly in pattern knitting where rows need to be reset. By the time you are ready to knit once more, the carriage may have clocked up quite a few extra rows.

6
PRACTICE·MAKES·PERFECT

PRACTISING anything has an unpleasant hint of the disciplines of childhood you may well want to forget. However I'm saying it here with confidence, because you so quickly achieve perfection in machine knitting that interest in the craft increases the more you practise. The little bits and pieces you need to learn before you set to and make your first sweater are fundamental to all garment knitting. Once you have learned them they can be varied to suit your requirements. Mistakes will be made; knitting will fall to the floor, stitches will drop, yarn will wind itself around the brushes; but by the time you have produced these samples so that they look neat and professional you will also have learned why you made mistakes and how to put them right. What is even more important, you will have learned how to avoid them. You should also enjoy fiddling with the machine and learning to control it.

If you can conquer the hems or welts at waist, cuff and neckline, all that remains is the straightforward knitting of front, back and sleeves. Practice will already have shown you that this is the easiest and quickest part, since the machine eats up the length in no time.

Even if you have or intend to buy a ribber, it is important to know how to make these hems. You will not always want to start a garment with a rib; a jacket, for example, or a traditional baby's matinée coat would need neat hems. Once you know these techniques and begin to design for yourself you will find ways of adapting the principles learned as you develop ideas. In some respects lack of a ribber can be a good thing – you are not likely to sit bemoaning its absence and blaming any non-productivity on this, rather you will arrive at a stage when you will be proud of your achievements without one. You will either decide that it really isn't necessary to buy one after all, or you will feel ready for one technically and eager to explore all the stitch variations which double bed knitting presents. Of course you may decide that machine knitting is not an obsessive interest and the amount you do does not justify the extra expense of the ribbing attachment, so it's good to have convinced yourself that you can produce lovely knitwear without one.

A careful study of the garments in specialist knitwear shops will show that some of the work done on home knitting machines – the label will often say 'hand framed' – will have 'continental' ribs. It is true to say that this mock rib is gradually becoming less acceptable as the 'knitwear revolution' continues to grow. As more designers translate their fashion ideas into yarn the competition gets harder. The young designer has to be able to afford a ribber if ribs are fashion news. At the time of writing, the knitwear fashion shows are full of fisherman's knits, ribbed shawl collars, rib skirts and garments with a hand knitted look, often produced on chunky machines.

However, the world of high fashion is probably not your prime concern. You are more likely to be making garments for family and friends or perhaps setting up a small business locally. This doesn't mean that the work you do will not be design-conscious both in colour and shape, but it does mean that it is not necessary to have every last gadget available in order to knit, and also to earn should you want to, very successfully.

· Some practice pieces ·

For the instructions that follow, knitters on the larger gauge machines will need to adapt yarn and tension, but the method will be the same. I have included a method for producing a true rib on these machines, since mock ribs and hems are often too bulky for certain styles of garment. This ribbing method can of course be worked on standard gauge machines if you have time and patience. Practice of these simple pieces will soon make you perfect, helping you towards an understanding of your machine's function. Once this is mastered, together with the understanding of tension, you will be able to design garments for yourself.

Use a light coloured 4 ply equivalent yarn if possible, it is much more sympathetic to a nervous beginner. Tensions given are for this type of yarn. The waste yarn should be similar but of contrasting colour. Follow your instruction book for open-edge cast on as this varies from one machine to another, depending on whether or not there is a cast-on comb. When using the nylon cord in the casting-on sequence, the first row of knitting is sometimes unsuccessful. The yarn does not form a stitch but curls up out of the needles above the sinkers. A stronger downward pull on the cord whilst knitting the first row should rectify this, but if the problem persists, then take the tension down a whole number, or until the first row knits satisfactorily. After you have worked the hem, continue knitting and practise increasing and decreasing, finally casting off with the latch tool or eyelet tool.

For the two hems with picot and tuck stitch edges instructions are given for both non-automatic and automatic machines, but first practise a straightforward hem.

· The plain hem ·

Cast on 40sts with WY, T5 (approx)
K 7 or 8rs ending at R of machine. Remove yarn from the feeder
Set carriage to slip (part, or free move) but not to pattern. Move carr across sts to L side – the needles remain stationary and do not knit

Set carr for normal knitting
K 1r with nylon cord, T8, carr at R
Set RC to 000
With MY:
K 1r T8
K 10rs T4
K 1r T8
K 10rs T4
K 1r T8
Carr at L, RC 23

To turn up the hem Using the eyelet tool, hook up the stitches of the first loose row (T9) onto the corresponding needles. As you hook up the stitches pull the needles right out to the holding position. This is quicker, and ensures that the stitches you have hooked up stay

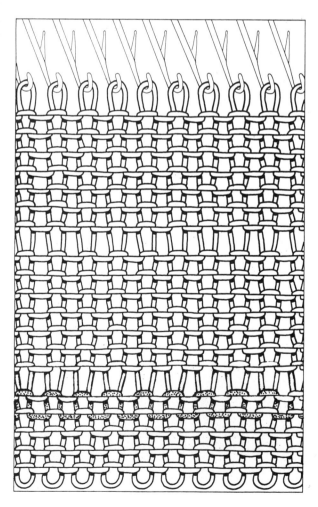

The rows on loose tension will ensure your hem lies flat

50

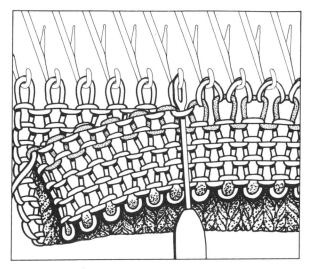

Turning up the hem

safely on the needles. You may find that the work curls up, making it difficult to keep the knitting in the needles. I always hang the claw weights in the back of the work, anchoring them evenly in the back of the last set of rows knitted on tension 4.

Set the carriage to knit normally
K 1r T10

Transfer the weights to the front of the work and carry on knitting in main tension – probably tension 6 – practising increasing and decreasing as shown in Chapter 3. Remember to knit your final row before casting off on the largest tension your machine is capable of – probably tension 10 – otherwise your casting off edge will be too tight whether done with the eyelet tool or the latch tool.

The rows you work on the loose tension – tension 9 – delineate the hem. The stitches of the first and last rows need to be loose, and the

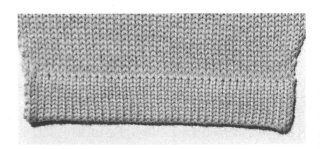

The finished hem gives a neat edge to a sweater

final joining row even looser, otherwise the hem will not lie flat. The edge of the hem is worked on a loose tension to allow for the fold of the knitted fabric. If you ever work a hem without observing these tension rules, or do them on a tension which is not large enough, you will realise how important they are – no amount of pressing will induce a hem to lie flat if this rule isn't followed.

· Hand cast-on hem with tuck stitch edge ·

If your machine is electronic or automatic, insert the card which will give you the 1×1 or birdseye pattern (one stitch main colour, one stitch contrast alternating along the row). Before you start knitting, lock the card in place. There is no need to join the ends with the plastic snaps since the card will not be required to move. See your instruction manual for inserting and locking the card.

Hand cast on as follows:

Carr at R, using 1×1 pusher, bring out 20 alt Ns to HP over 40Ns. Leave rem Ns at NWP. It will be necessary to have 2Ns at WP at one end, it does not matter which

With MY in the feeder, and a 'tail' of yarn three times the width of the needles, 'e' wrap loosely as follows:

Take the end under the first needle on the right and wrap it clockwise around the needle, bringing it round and then under the second needle from the right and so on to the last needle at the left

RC 000, T4

Now, with carriage set to knit, knit carefully across to the left. The needles knit back to working position. If they won't knit back you have wrapped too tightly. If they stay at holding position you have forgotten to set the carriage to knit.

Now bring all the needles out to holding position, knit to right. Knit two or three rows, bringing the needles out to holding position and knitting them back on each row until you can insert the cast-on comb if you have one, or hang the weights easily. Then you no longer need to take the precaution of using holding position to ensure the stitches will knit.

K to RC 11; carr at L

Automatic machines: Set pattern according to the instructions for your machine

K r12, carr at R. The pattern is in the memory, or the needles have been selected, according to the make of your machine

Leave the card locked

Set carr to tuck and tuck 3rs. RC 15, carr at L

Non-automatic machines: Bring EON out to HP using 1×1 pusher

Set carr to hold

K 3rs, carr at R

All machines: Set carr to K

K 14rs T4, carr at R

K 1r T8

To turn up the hem

Preferably using the double eyelet tool, pick up the front strand of the cast-on 'chain' onto the right hand eyelet, the back strand onto the left. You will need a bit of practice to become adept at this technique, so use the single eyelet tool if you find it difficult at first. Bring the needles out to holding position as you do this. It is a more continuous action, and ensures the stitches stay on the needles.

K 1r T9, carr at R

You will see from these two hems that you can choose whichever cast-on method you prefer, but if you use the hand cast on, the facing – that is the first set of tight tension rows you knit before the fold row – needs two rows less than the hem itself. When turned up, the tucks on the fold line form a mock picot effect. A true picot can be worked by hand, or with the lace carriage if your machine has one.

When turned up the tuck rows form a picot effect at the edge of the hem

The true picot worked with the lace carriage or by hand transfer

· Picot hem using lace carriage or by hand transfer ·

If using the Knitmaster machine with lace carriage, the whole hem can be knitted with this.

Cast on 40sts using WY, T5 (approx)

K 7 or 8rs, ending with carr at R of machine

If using the nylon cord:

Remove yarn from the feeder

Set carr to slip (part or free move), but not to pattern

Move carr to L (the needles remain stationary and do not knit)

Set carr for normal knitting

K 1r with the nylon cord, T8, carr at R

Set RC to 000

With MY:

K 1r T8

K 8rs T4

K 1r T5, carr at R, RC 10.

Using a lace transfer carriage on Brother, Toyota and Singer machines:

Move lace carriage across sts L to R. All Ns are selected. Lace carr at R

With 1×1 pusher, push every second N back to WP

Move lace carr across Ns to L, the sts are transferred

Check that all sts have transferred successfully. Ns will again be selected but this does not matter, they will knit back to WP on next row

Release lace carr from machine

Manual transfer:

Transfer every other stitch onto the needle next to it, using the single eyelet tool. Make sure both end needles have a stitch on them.

Leave the empty needles at working position
K 9rs T4
K 1r T8, RC 22
Turn up the hem by lifting the stitches of the first loose row after the nylon cord onto the corresponding needles
K 1r T9, carr at L
Experience has shown that the hem lies flatter if the facing has one row less than the hem front. The stitches transfer more easily and the picot looks better if the row on which the transfer will take place is on a looser and more accommodating tension.

The picot edge, whether achieved with the lace carriage, by hand transfer or by tucking, can soften and add an understated detail to an otherwise plain sweater.

Hems are often necessary at the end of the knitting, at the neck edge and also at the cuff where the sleeve has been knitted from the shoulder downwards. The same technique is used. This type of finishing is used on the sweater designs in this book. A plain finishing hem is given here. The edge can be varied by tuck, hand transfer or lace carriage.

An invaluable method of finishing necklines, and for sleeve edges when knitted downwards from the armhole edge

· A finishing hem ·

Cast on 40sts and knit a few rows, say 20, in MT6. End at R of machine
RC 000
K 1r T8
K 10rs T4
K 1r T8
K 10rs T4
K 1r T8, RC 32, carr at L
Hang the weights at the back of the work on the last group of rows on T4.
Turn up the stitches of the first loose row onto the corresponding needles of the final row,

pulling the needles out to holding position as you do so
K across all sts on T10, carr at R
Cast off with the latch tool
Sometimes the casting off can be too tight where the hem is for a neckline finish, particularly on a child's garment. This can often be rectified by working two rows of T10 before casting off. There are other methods of increasing the elasticity of the cast off which will be illustrated later in this chapter.

· Continental or mock rib ·

The continental or mock rib enables you to produce something on the machine that has the same appearance, if not the same elasticity, as true rib. The ribbed effect is achieved by leaving needles out of work, so that when the knitting is turned up to form a hem the spaces so formed, which would be filled by purl stitches in the true rib, close up, giving a ribbed look to the knitting.

Mock rib – a good compromise if you have no ribber

The two most usual needle arrangements used are 1×1 – that is one needle in working position and one needle at non-working position – and 2×1 – two needles in working position and one at non-working position. The latter gives a better result. One of the first sweaters I made was a 'skinny rib'. It should have been called a 'skinny mock rib' as the stitch set-up was four needles in working position and one at non-working position for the whole sweater. It proved to be very successful since I was then required to make several more for family and friends.

When using these needle set-ups you need to make sure there are needles in working position at each end of the work. If when designing a sweater this upsets the stitch calculations for the main knitting, you can adjust these on the turn-up row of the hem. You will notice that the tension is set finer than for the other ribs. Be liberal with your rows of waste yarn knitting before introducing the nylon cord. If the waste yarn is meagre there is a tendency for it to unravel as far as the main knitting, particularly if your tension is a little loose.

Over 41sts, using a 2×1 pusher, set up the Ns so that every third st is out of action at NWP and there are two stitches in WP at each end

Cast on using WY

K 10 or 11rs T3, carr at L

Break WY and knit in the nylon cord from the left, T8

With MY, RC 000, carr at R:

K 1r T8

K 20rs T3

K 1r T8

K 20rs T3

K 1r T8

Now bring the Ns at NWP to WP with the straight back of the pusher, lining them up with the Ns at WP on which you have been knitting, ready to turn up the hem

Before you start, have a look at the knitting you have just done. You could put the double eyelet tool into the pair of loops on your first loose row and lift them onto the corresponding needles of the last row. However if you do this it leaves an empty needle which will knit as you continue the main part of the work. As it originally had no stitch on it, there will be a row of holes on the turn up row. Most people have made this mistake at sometime or another, so if you do, console yourself that you are in good company. The way to avoid the holes is to put up the stitches in pairs, one to the left of the corresponding needles, so that

the empty needle is filled, and the one next to it is missed out, thus:

Turn up the hem and with the eyelet tool:

Hang first st on the R onto the second N on R

Hang the second st onto the first empty needle

Hang the third st onto the fifth N from the R

Hang the fourth st onto the next empty needle

Continue like this to the end, bringing all the stitches to holding position to keep them securely on the needles. This is not absolutely necessary, but I find it quicker and more secure than replacing each needle to working position after hanging the stitch on it

K across all Ns on T10

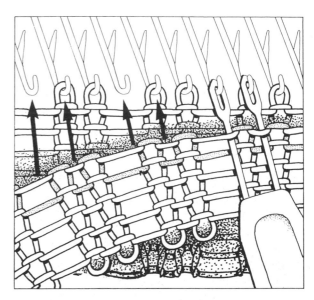

Turning up the mock rib

You can also finish the knitting with mock rib. Work the last row of the main knitting on a loose tension – probably T8 – then transfer your stitches ready to knit the hem. If you have knitted the front of a sweater and wish to make the neckband in mock rib, work the first loose row across the neckline stitches after the shaping is finished, and then transfer your stitches ready for the rib.

All these hems can be worked on any machine. Even if you own or intend to own a ribber it is still important to understand these methods, since they involve you in the construction and manipulation of knitting and stitches which will have many applications in other contexts such as pocket edgings, piping trims and so on. They can of course be worked on the bulky or chunky machines in the thicker yarns, but since these thick yarns can often make the hems out of proportion to the main garment, it is better to form a true rib on the larger gauge machines.

· Ribbed welts for chunky machines ·

In the absence of a ribber, the easiest solution is to start with a closed cast-on edge, knit the required depth of hem and convert it from stocking stitch to rib by dropping the necessary stitches and picking them up with a latch tool. This may sound laborious, but as with everything else you are learning on the machine, you quickly become quite skilled at it, and able to whizz the stitches back up the knitting to form knit stitches and construct any form of rib hem you want: K1, P1; K2, P2; and so on. It is certainly quicker than knitting the ribs by hand.

No one would know this rib was worked with a latch tool

Bring out 20Ns to HP, carr at R, set carr for normal knitting (not hold)
Cast on by hand – 'e' wrap – quite loosely. The end you wrap should be about three times the width of the Ns
Set RC to 000

With the tension two whole numbers less than MT, probably T3 if using a double knitting yarn which knits stocking stitch nicely on T5, knit carefully across the first row. If the carriage refuses to knit, you have wrapped too tightly, so start again. You will find that however sympathetically the yarn has been wrapped, the first stitch tends to pull tight in the needle, and may not knit properly in spite of tension adjustments. To remedy this, ease the yarn through the feeder as you begin to knit the row, and check both end stitches for the first couple of rows.

Insert the comb and hang the weights after the first row. If your machine has no comb bring the needles out to holding position and with your carriage set for normal knitting, knit them back to working position over the first three or four rows until you hang the weights.
K to RC 10

For a K1, P1 rib

Starting at the right, drop the second stitch in from the edge, letting it run down the knitting for nine rows. Always make sure it drops one row less than the number of rows you have knitted. You will spoil the cast-on edge if you lose the first row stitches. Now take the latch tool and pick up the dropped stitch. You have a ladder of yarn above this, which you climb by pulling each strand in turn through the stitch on the latch tool. When you arrive at the top, replace the stitch on the needle. For K1 P1 rib drop every other stitch. (For a K2, P2 rib drop every other pair of stitches.) Knit several rows MT5, finishing with one row of T8, with the carriage at the right. Cast off with the latch tool. It is important to work this technique stitch by stitch rather than to prepare the whole welt in advance for the latching up technique, since you need to control the number of rows the stitch is allowed to run down.

When you have taken the work off the machine, pull the welt vertically to help the re-formed stitches to fill out. They will continue to relax and settle for an hour or so after you have finished. You should aim to produce a firm, springy rib with plenty of elasticity. The

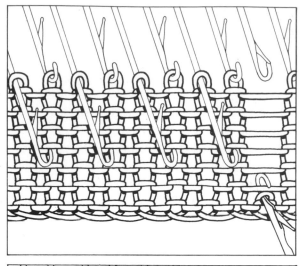

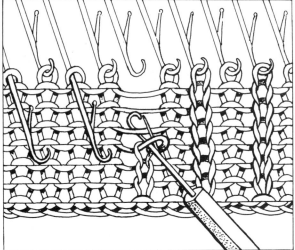

Dropping and latching up the stitch to form the rib

knitting yarn, so you will need to alter them proportionately to suit whatever yarn you are practising with.

Let's say the MT is at 5 and you have knitted about 10 rows:

K 1r T7
K 5rs T3
K 1r T7
K 5rs T3
K 1r T7

Drop and work the stitches singly as before. When all have been worked, turn up a hem by lifting the first row of loose tension stitches onto the corresponding needles

K 1r T10

Cast off with the latch tool

Pull the rib vertically to settle the stitches. The knitting will take an hour or so to relax sufficiently for the fold row to perform its function.

Although designed for chunky machines, this technique can be worked on standard gauge machines by those with no ribber and a lot of patience!

· The use of holding position ·

This was discussed in Chapter 3, and along with the use of waste yarn, it is something which newcomers to machine knitting find particularly baffling. It is not until you have actually used needles in holding position that you begin to see how it works. Probably the first use you will make of this carriage setting is for neckline shaping, and the technique is sometimes called 'short row shaping' or 'partial knitting'.

You can of course shape the neck of a sweater by casting the stitches off, but this method has several inadequacies. Firstly the cast-off edge, however neatly and loosely you have managed to do it, remains inflexible when it comes to pulling a round neck over the head, or trying to do so. Having cast off, you then have to go to the trouble of picking up the stitches you have just disposed of in order to knit the neckline and trying to do this neatly and evenly can sometimes defeat even the most experienced knitter. Moreover, it is a slower

potential for this varies with different types of yarn and it is essential to experiment.

· Finishing in rib ·

This can be practised on the same piece you have worked the rib on at the beginning. If you wish to finish with a rib, at the neck or wrist for example, knit the rows to be ribbed two whole numbers less than the main tension, working the last row, which will be the cast-off row, at least two whole numbers larger. Be careful not to exceed the rows for the rib when you drop the stitches down. Neckline ribs are often doubled over, which gives a comfortable looking finish to a chunky-knit sweater. Again the tensions given are for the average double

process than using holding position, and can only be recommended when unavoidable, as for example when the lace carriage is being used, which on some machines will not pass over needles which are at holding position. Where possible, therefore, a method of shaping the neck and at the same time holding onto the neckline stitches in order to knit the neckband on them is neater, quicker and easier.

The final turning up and casting off of the little hem which forms the neckband can still give an opening which tends to be ear damaging when pulled over the head simply because the cast-off row is inflexible. This is a particular problem where children's clothes are concerned, but there are two ways around it which will be shown later.

Before attempting the neckline, it is a good idea to fiddle about with your machine, without any yarn in the feeder, bringing needles out to holding position, setting the carriage to knit so that they all return to working position, bringing half of them out to holding position, setting the carriage to hold, and observing how those needles remain at hold until the carriage is set for normal knitting, when they return to working position.

Practise the use of holding position with this sample piece:

Thread up your yarn tension unit with two contrast yarns, Col 1 and Col 2.

Cast on with Col 1 60sts, 30 to L and 30 to R of centre 0, tension to suit yarn – say T6 for the practice arcylic

K 12 or 13rs ending with carr at R

Change yarn in feeder to Col 2

* Set carr to hold

Bring out 10Ns at L to HP

K 2rs, carr at R. The 10sts at L have not knitted

Bring out another 10Ns at L to HP

K 2rs, carr at R. There are now 20sts at L which have not knitted

Continue like this until, with carr at R, only 10sts at R remain at WP

Set carr for normal knitting

K to L. All the needles have now knitted back to WP

Break yarn and thread feeder with Col 1

Set carr to hold

Bring 10Ns at R to HP

K 2rs, carr at L

Continue like this until, with carr at L, only 10sts at L remain at WP

Set carr for normal knitting, K to R. All the Ns have now knitted back to WP

Break the yarn and thread the feeder with Col 2 and repeat from * as many times as you wish finishing at R and ready to join in Col 2, but don't remove the knitting from the machine.

Using two colours helps you to understand how holding position works

Changing the colour helps you to understand what is happening to the knitting when you shape in short rows. The piece you have just knitted should be rectangular, if all has gone well. However there are instances when you might want one side of the knitting to be wider than the other, if it is to be the hemline of a sideways-knitted skirt for example. In this case the techniques is as follows:

Finish your last section at R

With Col 2 in the feeder, K several rs ending at R

* Change to Col 1 and K 2rs

Set carr to hold

Bring out all Ns, except 10 at R, to HP

K 2rs

Replace next 10sts to UWP

On a larger scale this method of short row shaping is perfect for knitted skirts

K 2rs – the Ns at UWP have knitted, you now have 20sts at WP on the right
Replace next 10sts to UWP
K 2rs – 30sts at WP at R
Continue until all sts are at WP and carr is at R
Bring 10 Ns at L to HP
K 2rs
Bring next 10 Ns at L to HP
K 2rs
Continue until only the last 10sts at R rem at WP
Set carr to knit
K 2rs
Change to Col 2 and K 6rs
Repeat from * two or three times more until you feel you understand what you are doing

You will find that where you 'turn' in the row, that is at the point between the last needle of holding position and the first one at working position, a small hole forms. If you have practised the method and understood it, then you won't find it too difficult to 'wrap' the yarn around the needle at holding position before the carriage returns to the side of the work. This eliminates the hole but is laborious. A better solution is detailed below, and whoever the unknown knitter is who devised the quick answer to this problem deserves an accolade.

If you have just finished a complete section, having knitted six rows of Colour 2, start again from *, shaping in groups of ten needles as before, but arranging the needles in the following way:
* Change to Col 1 and K 2rs, carr at R
Set carr to hold
Bring out all Ns except 11 at R to HP
K to the L
Bring the 11th N from R out to HP
K to the R, 10sts are in WP
Replace next 11sts to UWP
K to the L
Bring the 21st N from R out to HP
K to the R, 20sts are in WP
Continue like this, replacing 11sts to UWP, knitting to the L, bringing the last st knitted back to HP and knitting to the R until all the sts are at WP and carr is at R. If you look at your needles as you are knitting you will see that the yarn wraps itself over the 11th needle when this is replaced to UWP and the carriage is taken back to the right.
Now bring 9Ns at L to HP
K to the L
Bring the tenth N from the L to HP
K to the R
Bring the next 9Ns at L to HP
K to the L
Bring the 20th N from L to HP
K to the R
Continue until only the last 10sts at R remain at WP
If you look at your needles again you will see that the yarn has wrapped itself over the tenth needle of each shaping group when this is brought out to holding position and the carriage is taken back to the right.
Set carr to knit
K 2rs
Change to Col 2 and K 6rs
Repeat from * as before
This method is a little confusing at first, but well worth knowing, and a very quick technique to perform compared to hand wrapping the yarn.

To hand wrap the yarn when short row shaping The wrapping technique can be done

manually but adds considerably to your knitting time. Your pattern would read as follows:
Bring 10Ns at L to HP
K to the L
Now take the yarn under the last N at R in HP
K to the R . . . and so on.
When you replace the groups to upper working position the principle is the same, the yarn is always taken under the first needle in holding position next to the last knitted stitch, before the carriage returns to the edge of the knitting.

Words of warning about your technique as you knit Remember to move your weights as required as shaping alters the balance of your work. Give particular attention to the point where the needles at holding position meet those at working position. Sometimes the first stitch at working position does not knit, or the first three or four are missed. It's nearly always a question of weighting the work in the correct place in order to rectify this.

When working partial knitting it is not necessary to take the carriage across all the needles in holding position, you only need to clear the one that is next to the needles in working position before returning the carriage to the side of the work. However the beginner tends to be more extravagant with the knitting action and this often causes trouble in the form of loops of yarn, which even if they don't wrap themselves around the brushes and immobilise the carriage need to be dealt with by pulling out the row and doing it again. However careful you are not to take your carriage too far over and to manually check the tension of your yarn through the feeder, things will go wrong occasionally and it is better to do the rows again than to try to darn in loops afterwards.

If you have several grammes each of a variety of colours in yarn of a similar thickness it can be great fun experimenting with shape and colour using the holding technique. One of my first practice pieces became a cushion. I had quite a bagful of small amounts of Shetland yarn so I waxed and wound these, cast on 120 stitches and simply experimented, shaping sometimes in groups of fives, tens,

fifteens or twenties. The edges were not particularly even, because I went rather wild and put lots of random wedges of colour here and there without worrying about balancing the rows at right and left, but this irregularity was eliminated when the cushion was made up. A plain stocking stitch piece was knitted as a back, and as neither piece had been made to an exact size or shape this had to be superimposed when the two pieces were sewn together.

· Almost your first sweater ·

The next practice piece is quickly knitted, and is a simple and invaluable exercise since it embodies the techniques and methods already discussed. It means in fact, that once you understand how to apply tension to your knitting you are on your way to designing for yourself in any yarn you choose. However don't worry about garment tension just yet. If you are using an acrylic yarn as advised, the stitch tension given here should be satisfactory and the little sweater you produce may fit someone's teddy bear!

The pattern is presented in two ways, one diagrammatic and the other written instructions. Pattern books nowadays always have a diagram of the garment with the measurements printed and shaping instructions included. These are invaluable, especially if you are not using the yarn recommended. Even if you are, it means you don't have the often fruitless struggle to obtain the tension given, but can adapt the pattern to the tension measurements you choose. If you are not used to following a diagram and are more at home with the printed word you will find it worth your while to make the change. It is so much easier once you become familiar with it and by far the best method for recording your own patterns. Read the instructions through completely before beginning and try to relate them to the diagram as you do so.

· Small sample overblouse ·

Yarn: Your 'practice' yarn, probably 4 ply equivalent acrylic

Tension: MT7

Front

Cast on 66sts

K a 12r hem (practise one from the samples)

After turning up, with the carr at R:

RC 000, MT 7

K to RC 60

To shape armholes: Cast off 6sts at beg of next 2rs

Hang a weight at the edge of the work to prevent tight cast-off sts

54sts rem, RC 62

K to RC 88, carr at R

To shape right side of the neck Set carr to hold

Bring out 31sts at L to HP

K to the L

Wrap the yarn around the last N at HP on R

K to the R

Bring out the next 3Ns to HP

K to the L

Wrap the yarn around the last N at HP at R

K to the R

Repeat the last two rows four times more finishing with carr at R

8sts rem at WP, RC 100

Break MY

With WY in the feeder K 8rs, carr at R

Break yarn

You have now finished shaping the right side of the neck. If you get into a muddle with this short row shaping, it is easy to count the number of shapings you have done by looking at the groups of stitches in holding position. Each third stitch will have yarn wrapped over it.

If you need to unpick, replace holding position needles to working position first. Remember to adjust your row counter *every time you unpick a row*. If you feel you can cope, wrap the yarn automatically. In this case you would bring 30 stitches to holding position, knit to the left, then bring needle 31 out to hold before knitting back to the right. The rest of the shaping would be worked by bringing out two needles to holding position, knitting to the left, and bringing the third needle out before knitting back to the right.

To shape left side of the neck With the carr still set to hold, and no yarn in the feeder, move it over Ns to the L side of the work

The R shoulder sts on WY will drop off the Ns; replace Ns to NWP

Fold these stitches to the back of the work and hang a weight to fix them there. This prevents them catching in the brushes as you finish the rest of the knitting

Now replace 23sts at L to UWP

Reset RC to 88, MY in feeder

K to R

Wrap yarn around last N in HP

K to L

Bring out next 3Ns to HP

K to R

Wrap yarn around last N in HP

K to L

Repeat last two rows four times more, finishing with carr at L

8sts rem at WP, RC 100

Break MY

With WY in the feeder K 8rs, carr at R

With the carriage still set to hold and no yarn in the feeder, move it over the Ns to the R. The sts will drop off the Ns, and should be folded and weighted as for the right side to keep them out of harm's way.

Replace 8 shoulder sts to NWP

If you wish to wrap automatically, replace 24 stitches at the left to upper working position, knit to the right. Bring the last stitch knitted back to working position, knit to the left. Finish the rest of the shaping as for right side.

Neckband

Bring an extra N out to HP at each end of the centre 38 Ns (this helps when sewing up the neck hem)

Set carr for normal knitting and work a small hem:

K 1r T8

K 6rs T4

K 1r T8

K 6rs T4

K 1r T8

Pick up the corresponding stitches of the first loose row with the eyelet tool. (Practise doing two or three at a time, bringing the needles out to holding position as you work them – this is much quicker than resetting them back to working position.)

When all have been picked up:

K 1r T10

Cast off with the latch tool

Back

Work as for the front as far as RC 88

K 4rs, RC 92

To shape the right side of the neck Set carr to hold

Bring 31sts at L to HP

K to L

Wrap yarn around last N at HP at R

K to R

Now bring out the next 5Ns to HP

K to the L

Wrap the yarn around the last N at HP on R

K to R

Repeat the last 2rs twice more

8sts remain at WP

Put these on waste yarn as before

Work the left side to match following the method described for the front, and work the neckband to match

Joining the front to the back at the shoulders

Bring 8Ns to WP

With the right side of the work facing, replace 8 shoulder sts onto the Ns. The WY will be at the front of the work. Don't bring Ns out to HP

Now with the wrong side of the other piece facing, replace the 8 corresponding shoulder sts onto the Ns, bringing them out to HP. The WY is at the back of this piece.

Before knitting the next row it is quite a good idea to pass the carriage, set to hold, over the needles. This presses the work together, making it easier to knit. The carriage rides more easily over the needles if the tension is set down to 2 or 3.

With carr at L, set for normal knitting, T10, K 1r

Cast off with the latch tool

Finish the other shoulder in the same way and remove waste yarn

Sleeves

Push up 60 Ns to WP. With the wrong side of the work facing, at the armhole edge hang the shoulder seam at centre 0, the under arms on N30 at either side, omitting the cast off stitches at the under arm. Now pick up evenly along the armhole edge approximately one stitch in from the edge. You will soon be able to do this quickly if you practise using the three-ended transfer tool for this purpose. Picking up three stitches, and missing one, should distribute the work evenly along the needles, adjusting as necessary and bringing the needles out to holding position as you do so.

Now is the time to get rid of a few ends and save on sewing time. Wherever there are ends that need securing along the armhole edge, weave them under and over 6 or 8 needles. It does not matter if the same needles have two or three strands on them. This method of weaving in ends is invaluable in multi-colour work. The ends are secured when you knit the first row of the sleeve, and are neatly trimmed when knitting is finished.

K 40rs

Work a finishing hem of 8rs

Pick up and work the other sleeve in the same way

Making up

Press according to the instructions, if any, on the yarn label, otherwise see information for pressing in Appendix 3. With right sides together, backstitch the cast off stitches at the armholes to the sleeve side edges, then back-stitch the underarm seams from waist to wrist, slip stitching the inside of the hems together. At the neck, carefully backstitch the seams of the neckband and slip stitch the inside seam. If there are any unsightly stitches where the shoulder seam joins the neck they can be eliminated by a bit of judicious swiss darning – using needle and thread to imitate the knitted

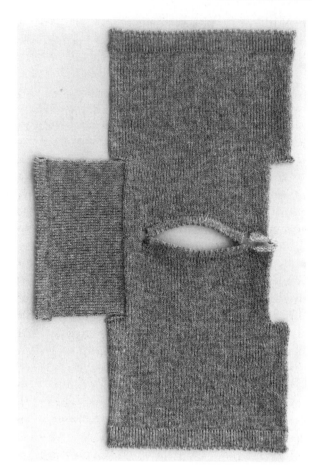

This small practice sweater shows how the work is organised. One shoulder has been joined on the machine and the sleeve stitches picked up along the armhole edge. The sleeve has been knitted finishing at the cuff. It only remains to close the other shoulder and knit the second sleeve

stitch. Finally, press seams on the wrong side.

Now you have learned the essentials of simple garment construction on the machine. This little item only needs to be scaled up to fit any size, and can be altered in many other ways to suit your requirements.

One problem that hits beginners almost immediately, especially when knitting for children, is neck size. If the neck is tight but needs to be only slightly slacker, then finishing with two loose rows before casting off with the latch tool may give sufficient play to draw the garment comfortably over the head. If this is not sufficient then there are two other methods which give a really flexible finish. Both methods increase the size of the cast-off stitch,

the first by using the sinkers, the second by stretching the stitch over two needles before casting off. Both are variations of casting off using the single transfer tool, which is described in your machine's instruction book.

· Casting off loosely, using the sinkers ·
Finish with the last row on T10, carriage preferably at left if you are right handed. Cast off using the single transfer tool, but transfer the stitches *behind* the sinkers, the yarn which is pulled through the stitches to cast them off goes in front of the sinkers as usual. The stitches can remain on the machine until the final one has been cast off and the work is then easily lifted off the sinkers.

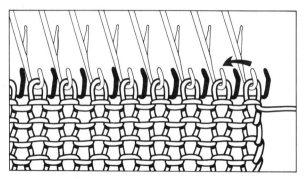

Casting off behind the sinkers avoids tight stitches

· 'Split stitch' cast off ·
This is less simple, more laborious, but even more elastic. It can also be used decoratively on the shoulder seam of a plain Guernsey-style sweater, where the seam is cast off on the right side of the work, and becomes a feature of the garment. Both methods are good, but this one is the better of the two.

Having knitted the final loose row on T10, with the carriage at the left, take the *right hand side* of the first stitch and transfer it to the next needle bringing that needle out to holding position as you do so using the transfer tool. Cast off. *The left side of the stitch remains on the first needle.*

Now take the right hand side of the new stitch and transfer it onto the next needle, bringing the needle out to holding position as

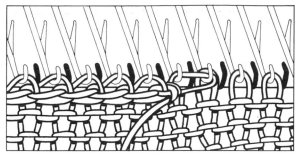

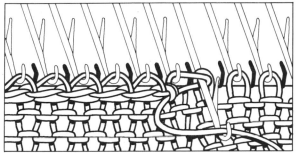

A perfect finish for the neckband of children's clothes or wherever maximum flexibility is required

you do so, cast off. Continue like this to the end, when you break the yarn and pull it through the final stitch.

Lift the work off the needles, or pass the carriage over them with no yarn in the feeder, on a low tension for ease of movement, to release the work from the machine.

Once you get going you will see that you are effectively lengthening each cast-off stitch by stretching it in front of the sinker and thus across two needles before drawing the casting off yarn through it and the stitch already on the needle. At no time is a complete stitch taken off a needle. This is not done until the final stitch is cast off, the yarn broken and pulled completely through it.

· Pockets and buttonholes ·

If you have diligently worked through these samples you will now realise that all things are possible on a knitting machine as far as garment design and construction are concerned. It will do whatever your ingenuity requires of it and if it happens to refuse, then it is probably only a question of altering the tension or choosing a different yarn to rectify the problem.

Not everyone has the ambition to design complicated or highly decorative knitwear. Your labours of love may manifest themselves in garments for the family; baby clothes, school jerseys, sweaters and cardigans, but inevitably some of these will have pockets – horizontal, vertical or diagonal – and button-holes. Many new knitters fight shy of knitting these and spend hours trying to add them to a garment after it is finished, whereas with a little forethought and planning they are much easier to incorporate in the garment as it is being knitted, and much neater too.

Careful consideration must be given to pocket placing on a garment. It is easy to do this if you study pocket placements on gar-ments you already have, and measure their positions in relation to hems, side-seams, and front openings. The width of the pocket opening and the depth of the pocket pouch should also be recorded. Here are a selection of samples for you to try. Adjust the main tension to suit your yarn, and the hem tensions to correspond. I have found it an advantage to knit the pocket pouch one whole tension number tighter than for the main knitting.

· Simple pocket for cardigan, jacket or waistcoat ·

These pockets are generally about 10cm/4in in width and depth on an adult garment.

Cast on 40sts T7

K several rs WY, change to MY

K 40rs ending with carr at R, break yarn

Bring 10sts at L and 10sts at R to HP

Set carr to hold

You are now going to work on the centre 20sts, making the pocket edge or hem first, then the pouch

With MY in the feeder, bring the end below the feeder up over the Ns in HP at R and then down to fasten securely to the right hand table clamp of the machine

Watch the knitting at all times, it tends to 'pile up' and needs careful weighting

K 1r T8

K 10rs T4

K 1r T8

K 10rs T4

K 1r T8

Turn up the work on the first loose row, picking up the stitches and putting them on the corresponding needles. Don't bring the needles out to holding position as you do so. The hem of the pocket lies at the back of the work

K 1r T10

Still watching the knitting carefully, and adjusting the weights every few rows, knit the pouch of the pocket:

K 40rs T6

K 1r T8

K 40rs T6, carr at R

Break yarn

Set carr for normal knitting, rejoin yarn at R

K across all sts

Continue knitting for about 20rs, T7 before breaking the yarn and removing the work from the machine.

If you press this carefully, you'll see that you can slip stitch the edge of the pocket hem to the main knitting keeping the vertical stitch continuity. The pocket lies flatter and looks neater if you do not catch in the hem facing. Oversew the edges of the pocket pouch.

Working a vertical pocket either at the side fronts or in the side seams is easy and makes a change from more conventional pocket placing

· Vertical pocket ·

Pockets can also be inserted vertically. The pocket slit is made by dividing the work and knitting each section of the main knitting separately for the required length. The hem and pouch are knitted afterwards.

Cast on 40sts

K at least 10rs T7, ending with carr at R

Now divide for the pocket opening:

Bring 20sts at L to HP

Set carr to hold

Finish R side first

Set RC to 000

K 40rs T7, break yarn

Bring these sts to HP

Carr still on hold, move it over Ns to L of work

Replace 20Ns at L to UWP

Join in MY at L

Set RC to 000

Finish the L side:

K 40rs T7, adjusting weights as necessary, carr at R

Holding position and a simple hem are the only techniques needed for this little pocket, knitted all in one with the garment

Set carr for normal knitting
K at least 10 more rows before removing the work from the machine. The pocket opening is complete

To work hem and pocket pouch With wrong side of the work facing, pick up 28sts along lower edge of the slit. In practice this would be the edge nearest the centre of a garment. Try to pick up along the same line of stitch edges.
Knit a small hem, starting with carr at R:
K 1r T8
K 6rs T4
K 1r T8
K 6rs T4
K 1r T8, carr at R
Turn up the hem as before
K 1r T10
Now knit the pocket pouch:
K 30rs T6
K 1r T8
K 30rs T6
K 1r T8, carr at L
Put sts on WY and release from the machine
Now arrange the pocket to see how the work is organised, and with the right side of the pocket pouch facing, replace the stitches onto the machine. The waste yarn will be at the front. With the wrong side of the pocket slit facing pick up 28 stitches neatly and evenly.
K 1r T10
Cast off with the latch tool
Slip stitch the sides of the pocket hem neatly to the garment, without catching in the facing, and oversew the edges of the pouch together.

A pocket in the side seam of a garment is worked in the same way, starting above the hem, and is obviously not quite so much bother as one set in the front of a jacket or waistcoat for example. If you are keen on standing around with hands in pockets, it's not so easy to slip your hands into these as they tend to be too far back for comfort. The design of the next sample, however, is for hands-in-pocket addicts.

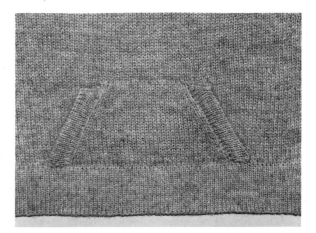

The 'kangaroo' pocket proves that anything is possible on a knitting machine

· Kangaroo pocket ·

The organisation of this pocket is a little confusing, but the actual knitting is probably easier than the so-called simple pocket.
Cast on 80sts
Knit a hem 20rs deep on T4, turning up on T10
Now put 20 stitches at each end of the work onto waste yarn. It does not matter at which side of the carriage you finished the loose row. If you ended up at the left, then bring 60 stitches at the right to holding position, set your carriage to hold and knit 20 stitches at the left in waste yarn – six to eight rows. Do the same at the right side of the work. Remember to push back the 20 empty needles at each side to non-working position. You now knit the pocket on the centre 40 stitches.
With MY in feeder, RC 000:
Decrease both ends of every third row ten times
20sts rem, RC 30. Put these sts onto several rows WY
With the wrong side of the work facing you, let the front of the pocket hang down on the machine side of the work. Pick up the 20 stitches from the loose row on waste yarn at the right hand side of the hem, 40 stitches from the loose row at the top of the hem (the base of the pocket front), and 20 stitches from the waste yarn at the right to give you 80 stitches.

K 30rs T7

With WY in feeder K several rs and release from the machine

With wrong side of work facing, replace the 20sts of pocket front onto the Ns

Then replace the 80sts of the garment body onto the machine and continue knitting for about 20rs

Release from the machine

Pocket hems Right pocket hem – hem of main knitting at R of machine, wrong side of pocket facing:

Carr at L

Pick up 22sts evenly and neatly along pocket edge, about 1st in on the smooth side of the knitting

K 1r T6, carr at R

K 6rs T4

Inc 1st at R and dec 1st at L on rs1, 3 and 5

K 1r T6, carr at L

K 6rs T4

Inc 1st at L and dec 1st at R on rs1, 3 and 5

K 1r T6

Turn up on the first loose row

K 1r T10, carr at L

Cast off with the latch tool

Left pocket hem – the shapings are reversed:

Garment hem at L of machine, wrong side of pocket facing, carr at R

K 1r T6, carr at L

Work the same as the previous edge, increasing at the left and decreasing at the right after the first loose row and after the second loose row increasing at the right and decreasing at the left

Press the pocket carefully according to yarn instructions

Slip stitch the hems of the pocket to the main knitting, omitting the inside edge

In practice you might wish to make this into two pockets, in which case you back stitch carefully up the centre line. The centre can be marked with a small length of contrast yarn after you have knitted the turn-up row – T10 – of the garment hem. To prevent precious pocket contents from falling out, the cast-off row of the pocket hem can be slip stitched to the main knitting for about 2.5–5cm/1–2in.

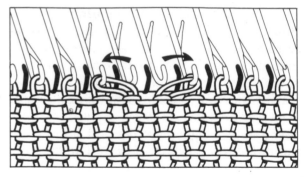

Small buttonhole:
a Transferring the stitches

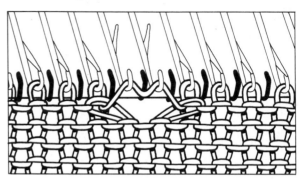

b Knit 1 row – loop of yarn on empty needles

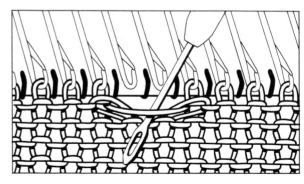

c Insert eyelet tool behind loop. Twist upwards and clockwise. Replace on needle. Repeat for second stitch

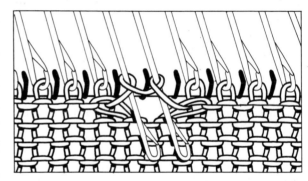

d Bring needles out to hold and knit back in the next row

· The small buttonhole ·

Small buttonholes can be worked by transferring stitches. Try a few on a piece of sample knitting. Transfer one stitch to the left and one stitch to the right on the buttonhole row, leaving the empty needles at working position. Knit one row. Now 'e' wrap the yarn that lies over the two empty needles and bring them out to holding position. Carry on knitting.

The small buttonhole is suitable for fine garments and children's clothes

Larger buttonholes for front bands of jackets and cardigans need careful placing. This is worked out by knitting the button band first. From that you can calculate the stitch width of the buttonhole and the number of stitches between each one, and place your buttonholes with total accuracy.

My favourite method for the front band of a jacket involves picking up the stitches for the band down the front edges. I prefer to do it this way because I like to have as little sewing up to do as possible. To knit a vertical button band can involve separately slip stitching band and facing to the garment and is a challenge to anyone who prides themselves on neatness.

Hand-finished buttonhole
a Bring the buttonhole needles forward so the stitches are behind the latches
b Lay a length of waste yarn across each set of buttonhole needles
c Knit each stitch back to working position by hand
d Continue knitting the hem. Buttonholes are worked to match in the facing

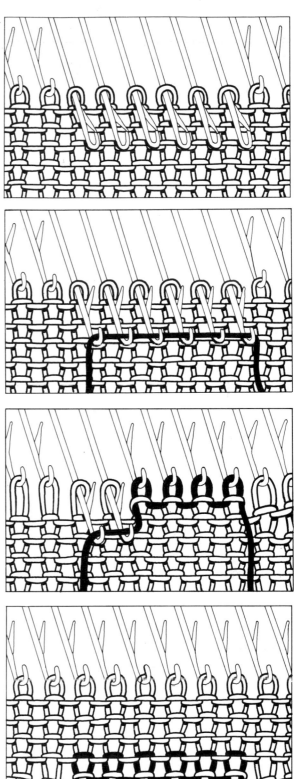

· Hand-finished buttonholes ·

To practise these buttonholes find one of your knitted samples, and with the wrong side facing pick up 40sts along the side of it.

K 1r T8

K 6rs T4, carr at L

Now set Ns for the buttonholes:

Leaving 3sts at either end of the work at WP, from the R bring out 6sts to HP, leave 8sts at WP, 6sts to HP, 8sts at WP, 6sts to HP

Using lengths of contrast yarn, knit the groups of 6sts for the buttonholes by hand, leaving them at WP

K 6rs T4, carr at R

K 1r T8

K 6rs T4, carr at L

Knit the buttonhole sts in contrast yarn as before

K 6rs T4

K 1r T8

Turn up the hem by picking up the stitches on the first loose row and putting them onto the corresponding needles

K 1r T10, carr at R

Cast off with the latch tool

Press the work according to yarn instructions.

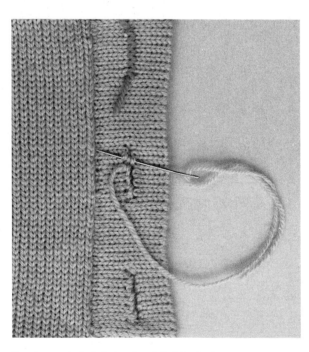

One buttonhole is being hand finished, the contrast yarn is still in the stitches of the other buttonhole

This 'fixes' the stitches. Carefully unpick the contrast yarn, and with the main yarn oversew the buttonholes through the stitches.

This method is successful with yarns which can be pressed, but it does of course mean that there is quite a bit of hand finishing to do.

· Machine-finished buttonholes ·

Buttonholes can be finished on the machine if you prefer and though the method is perhaps a little more complicated to understand it is well worth knowing, especially for yarn which cannot be pressed to fix the stitches. Persevere, follow the instructions carefully, and you will probably never do a hand-finished buttonhole again!

Pick up 40sts along the side of one of your practice pieces with MY

K 1r T8

K 6rs T4

Take three lengths of contrast yarn. Starting from either end of the work, hand knit the buttonhole stitches as for the hand-finished buttonholes

There are 3sts at either end and 8sts MY between each group of 6sts

K 6rs T4

K 1r T8

K 6rs T4

Now bring forward the three groups of needles on which you had worked the stitches in contrast yarn, plus one extra needle on the left of each group. They should be in upper working position, with the stitches just behind the latches. There are now seven stitches in each group (see diagram a opposite).

With the eyelet tool, pick up the stitches in main yarn above the contrast yarn – row 7 of the hem – into the needle hooks. It is important that the picked-up stitches are in the hooks and the stitches already on the needles just behind the latches. Now carefully pull the stitches in the needle hooks through the ones behind the latches. You are now ready to cast off these buttonhole stitches.

Working on the buttonhole stitches only, starting at R:

Transfer the st on N2 onto N1

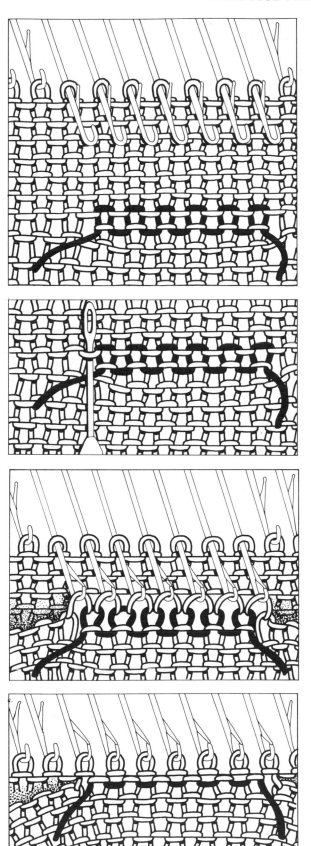

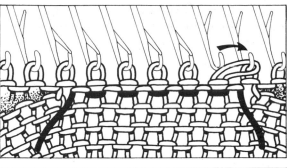

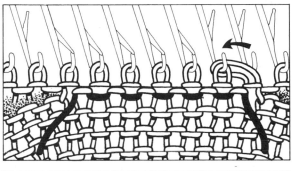

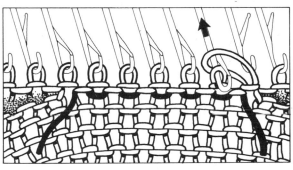

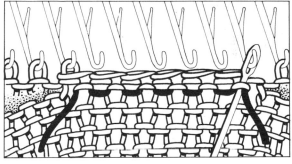

Working a buttonhole on the machine

a Bring out buttonhole needles to UWP, stitches just behind the latches, and one extra needle at the left

b Pick up bottom of first row of loops above contrast

c These loops rest in the needle hooks

d Draw each loop through the stitch behind the latch

e Transfer the second stitch from the right as shown

f Transfer both stitches back to the second needle

g Draw the second stitch through the first stitch and continue to cast off to the left

h Pick up the main yarn loops below waste yarn onto the corresponding needles. Carry on knitting

Transfer both sts back to N2

Carefully push N2 forward so that st1 only rests behind the latch

Bring N2 back to WP, drawing st2 through st1

Continue casting off in this manner until one stitch remains on the sixth buttonhole needle. Bring this needle forward so that the stitch rests behind the latch

Transfer st7 on L onto N6 and draw it through the stitch behind the latch

Now transfer it back to N7 on L

Leave all Ns in WP

The cast off is complete

To finish the buttonhole With the eyelet tool, pick up the buttonhole stitches below the contrast yarn – row 6 of the hem – onto the corresponding empty needles

K 6rs T4

K 1r T8

Turn up the hem

K 1r T10

Cast off with the latch tool

Carefully pull out the contrast yarn. The buttonhole is finished, and there is no sewing up to do!

Buttonholes in this method can be worked on vertical bands. These are knitted separately from the main work and attached to the garment afterwards either by hand or using the knitting machine. It is important to knit the button band first to establish the length required. The band is knitted in a continuous strip from neck to hemline and back. A loose row delineates the line of the hem. After the loose row there is a method of joining the front edge of the facing to the band as you knit:

Cast on 12sts

K 30rs T4, carr at R

K 1r T8

K 1r T4, carr at R

With single eyelet tool, pick up the edge stitch of the last row before the loose row, and put it on the first needle at the right

K 2rs

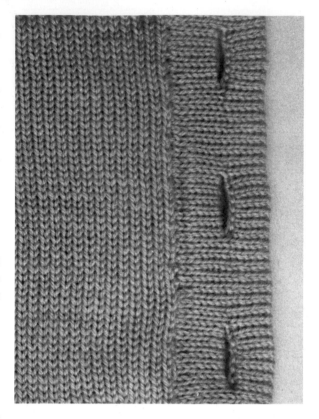

The finished buttonhole

Pick up the edge stitch of the third row before the loose row and put it on the first needle at the right

K 2rs

Continue like this, matching the rows correctly

In practice the buttons would be positioned evenly on the band, and the buttonhole positions calculated from this. You then have two techniques to work at once – the joining of the front edge of the band, and the buttonholes. This is not nearly as exhausting as it sounds, and it is very satisfying to have the buttonholes completed and the front edge closed by the time the knitting is finished. All that then remains is to join the front of the band to the front of the cardigan or jacket on the machine, and to slip stitch the facing into place.

7
THE·CHARTING·DEVICE

IT is not until you use a charting device that you realise how easy it makes garment design for the machine, yet it is possible to find quite experienced knitters who have the facility built into their machines, but who have never bothered to use it. 'It looks far too complicated for me' or 'it's such an unwieldy thing. I've never bothered to set it up' are frequent cries.

It is well worth the effort however. For those with lack of faith in their mathematical abilities it is a wonderful invention, while even those who find calculations simple, find it saves time. For all of us it makes garment knitting and shaping easier and more accurate. So if you have bought a machine with this facility, determine to use it.

If you have no charting device and cannot decide whether to purchase one, or whether you ought to buy a ribber first – a common dilemma amongst enthusiastic new knitters – the only answer is to make sure you eventually have both. Which comes first has to be a personal decision; I would now loathe to do without either, but I think the charting device may well be more important to me since I do a lot of work without the ribber.

Each make of machine calls the device by a different name, but whether yours goes under the title of Knitleader, Knitradar, Forma, Knit Tracer or Pattern Driver, its function is the same. It is a method whereby you insert a sheet with the drawn shape of your garment on it into an accessory at the back of your machine. A numbered rule in front of this will tell you how many stitches to cast on and the number of rows you will knit per centimetre is set by a dial or levers. The tripper is set so that every time the carriage passes it, the pattern moves up the required amount for the row setting. As the drawing of the garment moves, so you increase or decrease according to the position of the pattern line against the rule.

The setting for stitches and rows comes from the measurement of the tension square, so you can have a favourite pattern drawn on the pattern sheet and this can be used for any type of yarn you choose, in Fair Isle, lace, tuck stitch, or whatever stitch pattern you wish. All that is necessary is to knit the tension square in the stitch you are using for the pattern, according to the instructions with the device. You then select the appropriate rule for the measured stitches and set the dial or levers for the row measurement. The size of the sheet is either full scale, half scale, full width or half width. If it is half scale, then the original pattern has to be scaled down accordingly, easily achieved with the aids produced for the half scale devices.

Manufacturers produce a wide range of patterns specially for their charting devices, but the real joy of using this equipment is to be able to draw your own favourite shapes on it. Mine is most frequently used for trousers, the design for which was taken originally from a simple dressmaking pattern with no darts and a casing for elastic at the waist. Since the device for my particular machine has a full size clear pattern sheet on which the pattern is traced with a special pen provided – or any pen suitable for drawing on plastic surfaces which can be erased afterwards – I keep master copies of favourite and most used patterns on dressmaker's design paper, which is marked in centimetre squares, just as the charting sheet is. Using this, intarsia designs can also be planned and drawn ready for tracing and sizes

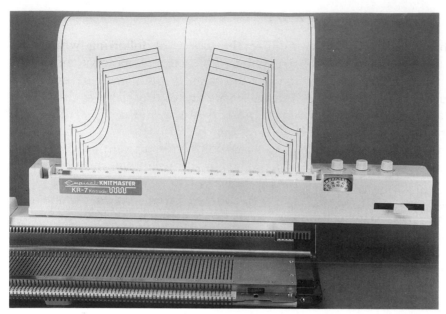

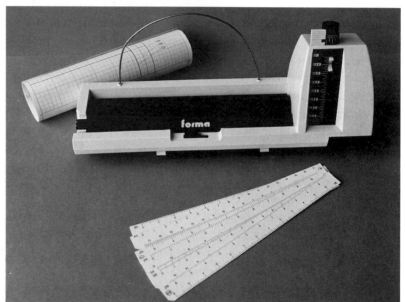

Designed to take the hard work out of knitting to size and to relieve you from tedious calculations, each machine has its own charting device; those illustrated include Knitmaster, Jones/Brother and Pfaff/Passap

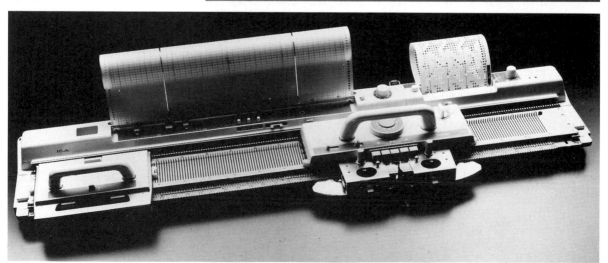

can be adjusted – all without any calculations whatever. The half scale and some half width sheets are made of paper making it unnecessary to make a master copy of your designs. Every time I knit a pair of trousers, with their irregular shaping, I appreciate how accurate the knitted shape the charting device produces is, and how difficult the calculations for it would be otherwise.

The charting devices for the Jones and Knitmaster machines also fit their chunky machines. This extends their utility and could influence your choice of machine if you are contemplating buying both a standard and a chunky machine.

It is important to remember that any mistake you have to correct must also be corrected on the charting device. If rows are unravelled then the pattern sheet must be turned back the appropriate number of times, and the tripper deactivated whilst the pattern is reset, otherwise the length of the garment will be affected. This also applies when knitting a 'v' neck. When the right side is finished and the work is recommenced at the 'v' point, it is better to deactivate the tripper until your carriage is at the left and you are ready to start knitting again, having made the appropriate manoeuvres if the pattern has to be reset.

Most of a busy knitter's problems arise when returning to the machine after an interruption of some description. If your mind has been on other things for some while a few minutes pass before knitting can be continued because you may have forgotten what stage you had arrived at in the pattern and have to calculate it again. With a charting device this never happens, leaving you to concentrate on the knitting without the worry of following written instructions. The current practice of giving pattern diagrams in both machine and hand knitting books makes it possible to draw these onto a pattern sheet and keep the written word to a minimum.

At some point in your knitting career you will encounter the term 'cut and sew'. This simply means you can knit jersey fabric to use for dressmaking. The most economical method of doing this is to draw or trace your dressmaking pattern onto the pattern sheet of your charting device, observing the directional arrows on the pattern pieces. Then square these pieces off into rectangles and knit these. You have far less waste fabric since each pattern piece will be cut from a piece no greater than its maximum width and length.

I once knew a knitter who never shaped on her machine. She was a clever dressmaker and her knitting machine and charting device were simply servants to this, producing endless jersey fabrics for dresses, coats and two piece garments and even contrast pieces for collar and cuffs. I was at a loss to understand why she never shaped the pieces on the machine instead of having to cut them after the knitting, but she simply enjoyed dressmaking more, and treated the knitting machine as an economical loom. I, on the other hand, love shaping on the machine. Nothing thrills me more than when something I have knitted comes out exactly the same shape and size as the pattern on the charting device, so I have never been a great enthusiast for 'cut and sew'. That a knitting machine with a charting device can satisfy both enthusiasms is a great testimony to its versatility.

DESIGN AND·MAKE

To design garments for yourself you must first become familiar with your machine, understand stitch tension, and be able to work out patterns to the size and shape you want from the information a tension square gives you. You can then knit sweaters in any yarn or combination of yarns you choose, and I hope the practical information in this book will help you to arrive at this point and give you the freedom to turn your mind towards knitwear design, namely the selection of colour, shape, yarn, and stitch pattern.

A feeling for these aspects of design develops subconsciously, and is an extension of your own preferences in colour form and texture, stimulated by your interests in the visual world and fed by your imagination. If you have a love of form and colour in nature, if you enjoy looking at pictures, tapestries, antique carpets, pottery and porcelain, for example, this will be reflected in the colour combinations, yarns, textures and stitch patterns you select for your knitting.

There is no set point of departure when designing a garment. You may fancy a particular shape first, and then decide on colour, finding a yarn and stitch pattern which bring all the aspects of your idea together in harmony. If you were inspired by a yarn first, you would then design a shape and stitch pattern to complement it. Though it is certainly a very proud moment when you produce a sweater that is all your own, by far the greatest fun for you as a designer is the run-up to the garment, as you select and discard ideas and knit the selection of samples from which you will make your final choice. You often hear knitters say, 'I could spend hours just playing with my machine!' They are excited and inspired by the potential of their machine and are knitting samples in different combinations of colours, yarns, and stitch patterns as ideas develop. The selection of yarns you need to be able to do this does not need to be too expensive, since you will be able to buy small amounts from oddment boxes and sales. As soon as you produce a sample you like make notes on the yarns used, stitch pattern and tension.

The working of the design can be from the information you record on your own drawn pattern, probably in a similar fashion to the one from my pattern notebook, or from a drawn pattern onto the chart of the charting device. You may also find ratio paper – a graph paper specially designed for knitters – is a help, since you can plan your design stitch by stitch using the tension information from your tension square. Ratio paper is particularly good for intarsia designs and for plotting shapings at armholes, underarms and sides.

It is a good idea to colour code pattern details; write in all your stitch measurements and the calculated stitches in red, for example, the rows in blue. Using this method I designed and made a simple stocking stitch sweater with amazing ease, and with less fear of error when knitting. The simple discovery of colour coding has now been absorbed into all my finished pattern writing.

On the facing page is a sheet from one of my pattern notebooks. It illustrates my method of relating specific information to the garment diagram when not using the charting device. The imperial measurements are a relic of my education, easily substituted with metric measurements if they are more familiar to you.

This method of pattern writing works well for me. I always enlarge any area with special information for easier reading – pockets, neckline, hem, welt details etc. My method of recording is not particularly neat, lines are not always straight, but the essential is there, and easy to see.

A pattern written like this assumes the understanding of the basic working techniques you will find fully explained in Chapter 6, 'Practice makes perfect'; for example both shoulders are left on waste yarn before finishing the neckband and garment sections are joined on the machine. So if any technique referred to in these patterns is unfamiliar, turn to Chapter 6.

Remember to read the pattern thoroughly and to relate it to the diagram before starting. Copy the diagram and write in all the necessary information. The simple shapes used here make it easy to alter yarns and therefore tensions, however for your guidance I have recorded the calculations worked from my tension squares, in the yarns which I used,

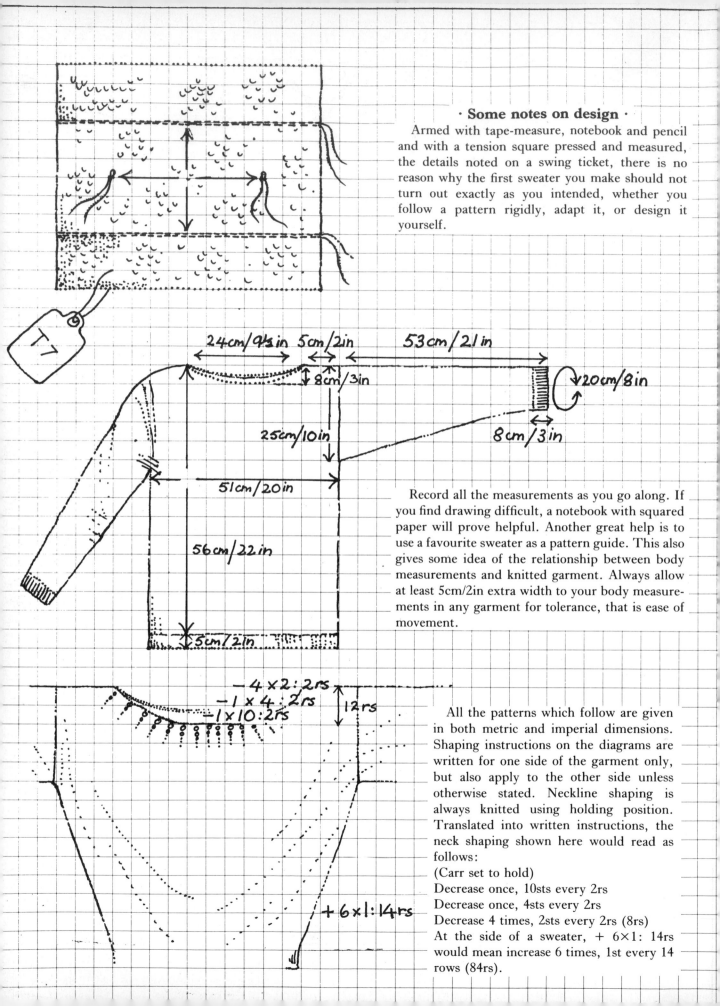

· Some notes on design ·

Armed with tape-measure, notebook and pencil and with a tension square pressed and measured, the details noted on a swing ticket, there is no reason why the first sweater you make should not turn out exactly as you intended, whether you follow a pattern rigidly, adapt it, or design it yourself.

24cm/9½in 5cm/2in 53cm/21in

8cm/3in

20cm/8in

25cm/10in

8cm/3in

51cm/20in

56cm/22in

5cm/2in

T7

Record all the measurements as you go along. If you find drawing difficult, a notebook with squared paper will prove helpful. Another great help is to use a favourite sweater as a pattern guide. This also gives some idea of the relationship between body measurements and knitted garment. Always allow at least 5cm/2in extra width to your body measurements in any garment for tolerance, that is ease of movement.

−4 × 2 : 2rs
−1 × 4 : 2rs
−1 × 10 : 2rs

12rs

+6 × 1 : 14rs

All the patterns which follow are given in both metric and imperial dimensions. Shaping instructions on the diagrams are written for one side of the garment only, but also apply to the other side unless otherwise stated. Neckline shaping is always knitted using holding position. Translated into written instructions, the neck shaping shown here would read as follows:

(Carr set to hold)
Decrease once, 10sts every 2rs
Decrease once, 4sts every 2rs
Decrease 4 times, 2sts every 2rs (8rs)
At the side of a sweater, + 6×1: 14rs would mean increase 6 times, 1st every 14 rows (84rs).

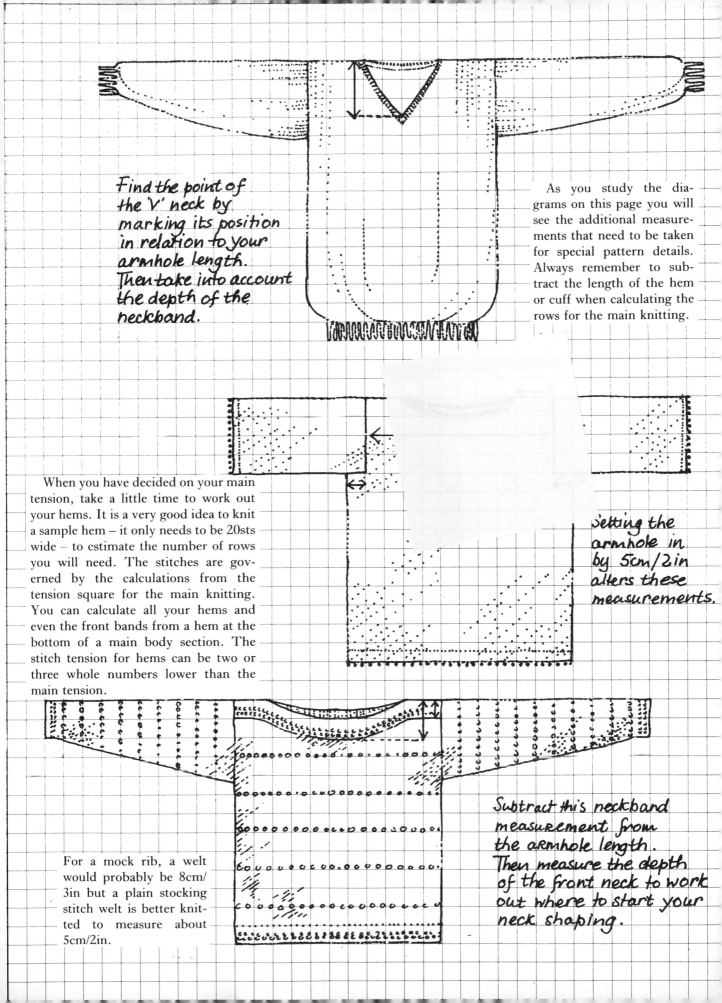

Find the point of the 'V' neck by marking its position in relation to your armhole length. Then take into account the depth of the neckband.

As you study the diagrams on this page you will see the additional measurements that need to be taken for special pattern details. Always remember to subtract the length of the hem or cuff when calculating the rows for the main knitting.

When you have decided on your main tension, take a little time to work out your hems. It is a very good idea to knit a sample hem – it only needs to be 20sts wide – to estimate the number of rows you will need. The stitches are governed by the calculations from the tension square for the main knitting. You can calculate all your hems and even the front bands from a hem at the bottom of a main body section. The stitch tension for hems can be two or three whole numbers lower than the main tension.

Setting the armhole in by 5cm/2in alters these measurements.

For a mock rib, a welt would probably be 8cm/3in but a plain stocking stitch welt is better knitted to measure about 5cm/2in.

Subtract this neckband measurement from the armhole length. Then measure the depth of the front neck to work out where to start your neck shaping.

As a keen beginner you will be baffled and tantalised by the variety and presentation of yarns produced specially for the knitting machine. As a result you may not feel confident to make changes in the yarn recommendation for a given pattern, or to experiment with them for your own designs. Since many of the yarns in your local machine knitting shop can be much cheaper than branded equivalents, usually without loss of quality, it is important to know how to use these.

The production of yarns for machine and hand knitting is a highly technical business and makes a fascinating study in itself. Professional yarn designers working for the large spinners marry technology to fashion, producing luxury yarns which are lovely to look at and to handle, and which have been purpose-designed from a technical viewpoint.

You will have noticed by now that whatever is being used to knit with is referred to as yarn. This is an umbrella term under which shelters any fibre which has been spun for any particular purpose – for tapestry, carpet weaving, woven fabric, hand or machine knitting, whether for industry or for home use. Those of us who have a hand knitting tradition are used to calling everything wool. After all, we have haunted the wool shops for years, for us

'wool' is the generic term. We have bought wool which is 70% cotton and 30% linen, mohair which is 100% acrylic, knitted a lovely silk jumper with wool we bought in a sale. Old habits die hard, but since there is now an enormous increase in interest and practice of the knitter's craft, both by machine and by hand, and thus a greater variety of the material to do it with, the term yarn is gradually becoming accepted and understood. Wool shops are becoming yarn stores, and to me the term conjures up the image of an Aladdin's cave heaped with exotica – yarns of every variety and mixture; natural yarn of every kind including the wools from all sorts of animals, not only the many breeds of sheep, but fox, alpaca and chinchilla; all types of synthetics and combinations of natural and synthetic.

In industry the word 'count' is used to indicate the thickness of the yarn. The count is based not only on the ply of the yarn but on the ratio of length to a given weight. It is a more accurate description than the terms 2, 3 and 4 ply, which hand knitters are so familiar with, which indicates the number of strands in the yarn but not necessarily its thickness. For example Shetland yarns are available in a 2 ply jumper weight and 2 ply lace weight – both are 2 ply, but are of very different thickness.

The yarn count is indicated by two numbers. The first number shows the number of strands or ends which are folded or plied together to make up the yarn. The second number represents the calculation based on the length of the yarn to a given weight. The larger this number, the finer the yarn. So if you look inside one cone and see 2/8 and another which reads 2/20 you will know that both have two ends or are two-fold (ie both could be called 2 ply) but that the second yarn is much finer than the first. Those figures are talked about as 'two eights', 'two twenties', 'two thirties' and so on. Often yarn catalogues give a minimum length per cone weight. As you become more experienced this can be a great help when calculating the quantity you require.

· Buying yarn ·

Specialist shops often purchase ends of ranges from the mills. These are yarns which have been spun for the commercial knitwear industry and are surplus due to an over-estimate of quantity for specific orders. The home knitter is given an inexpensive opportunity to knit with yarns specially designed to run smoothly through the machine and often in the colours and texture of current fashion trends. The problem is that these yarns are often so fine that as a beginner you may find yourself at a loss to know how to use them. The answer is that you simply use several ends together until they give a thickness of knitted fabric suitable for the particular garment you are going to knit. Of course when combining ends in this way, known as doubling, it is not necessary to have each end of the same colour, or even of the same yarn. The scope for designing a knitted fabric with blended colour and textural variety is enormous. Many of these industrial yarns are spun from luxury fibres such as angora, mohair, or cashmere and cost far less than their hand knitting counterparts, so your experimenting need not be too expensive.

Industrial woollen yarns are often sold 'in oil', meaning that the spinning oil is still in the yarn. You can smell it and feel it, and in fact it makes for easier knitting, but the fabric it produces is hard, open, and stringy. Its true character is only revealed once it is washed.

There is also a great variety of plain and fancy yarns available from specialist mail order yarn suppliers which are more expensive than from your shop, but which extend your choice. Most good catalogues give descriptions of the yarns and their uses to help you understand what you are buying. Compare the catalogue with what is available from your local shop. It would be expensive and pointless to buy yarn by post if it, or something very similar, is available there. You will generally find that someone on the staff has knitted samples of various yarns, or that garments have been knitted up, demonstrating how the yarn performs when different textures and techniques are used. The stitch tension used for the samples should be given and will help you to understand how the yarn behaves at various tensions, when doubled, using two or more ends, or with other yarns.

· Using hand knitting yarns ·

With the minimum of extra preparation you can use most hand knitting yarns on your machine. If it is a thick, fancy yarn with an uneven texture it will generally come into its own on the 200 needle machines in the weaving patterns, where it is not actually knitted, but is caught into the work by a finer main or backing yarn. As weaving is in part a hand technique, there is no need for a very fancy and irregular yarn to be put through the tension mast where it would flow erratically, or not at all. The ball of weaving yarn can sit on the floor at your feet. Some hand knitting yarns, however, are so textured that the weaving brushes cannot prevent the odd loop or knoppy bobble from entering the needle, which endeavours, without success, to knit it, causing the carriage to jam. If this occurs you have little choice but to accept that the yarn is unsuitable and try something not quite so troublesome in texture.

Owners of chunky machines should find it easy to knit with the fashion hand knitting yarns, though it can be a good idea to use a more conventional yarn for the hems at waist, neck, and cuffs if it suits the design.

Whenever hand knitting yarn is used through any machine it needs winding into a loose ball from which the end will flow smoothly and loosely from the centre. This is done on a wool winder. Furthermore as it is wound into this ball it needs to be waxed. This is a simple process whereby you hold the wax – a piece of candle will do – in one hand, allowing the yarn to run over it as you wind. The wax lays down the natural fibres of the yarn just sufficiently to allow it to run smoothly through the machine, and helps to prevent the fibres from being shed in the knitting process. The ball produced when waxing is very tight owing to the extra tension on the yarn as it runs over the wax. This can be felt when the end is pulled out from the centre – often the whole ball can be held up and suspended from this end. It therefore needs to be wound a second time to give a smooth, free-flowing supply of yarn to the machine.

Many machines have a little wax disc provided which sits on a stand on the tension unit. The yarn runs under this, and some knitters have it permanently on their machines, whatever yarn they are using. You will learn to judge whether the hand knitting yarn you are planning to use could benefit by extra waxing. There are also wax sprays on the market which some knitters find more convenient and just as efficient as the wax disc.

A skein holder is not used so much these days, as most hand knitting yarn is balled, and much more yarn is prepared ready for machine knitting. However it comes into its own when you are unpicking large pieces of knitting, which can be pulled out directly onto the skein holder. The skein thus formed is tied in two places with a contrast and colour fast or natural yarn, or even a piece of white string before removing from the holder. It can then be suspended above steam if this is possible, or quickly dipped in hand hot water, the surplus moisture lightly squeezed out, and hung up to dry. A gentle pull on the skein whenever you pass by helps to remove the kinks as it dries. It is then put back onto the skein holder and wound into balls, waxing in the process, rewound and is thus ready again for knitting on the machine. A word of warning when knitting up yarn recycled in this way; its texture will have been altered by the treatment it has been subjected to, and if you join it in half way up the back of a garment for example, it is bound to be noticeable. Keep it for ribs or hems. If you are working a Fair Isle pattern and it is the main colour, the design will generally disguise the changeover.

Sale time is a great time for the machine knitter to invest in a range of exotic hand knitting yarn for weaving purposes or for knitting on a chunky machine. Odd balls will do for intarsia work and are often the ends of ranges of luxury yarns which were too expensive for most hand knitters. You will soon be able to assess what your machine can cope with after a short and inexpensive period of trial and error.

All 200 needle machines will take hand double knitting yarns when knitted on every other needle. This means you have, in effect, converted your machine to a 100 needle machine, every other needle being out of working position for the whole of the design.

Whatever yarn you are using will flow through the yarn break more easily if placed on the floor at the back of your machine. This means that it is better to have the machine set up on a special knitting table rather than on any spare table you may have. Tension problems can arise where the yarn is simply set at the back of the machine, on the table where it can catch in the tools and the charting device very easily.

Some of the slippy yarns, notably rayons and fancy mixtures which, being heavy, long to unwind themselves into great loops on the floor whilst you are not looking, can be controlled by being placed in a plastic bag with the mouth of the bag simply squeezed closed by the hand, or fastened loosely with a wire closure.

ANGORA·SWEATER

This sweater couldn't be easier to make – it is a full size version of the practice sample in Chapter 6. Knitted in a beautiful combination of chinchilla and lambswool, the luxury of the yarn is fully revealed by the simplicity of the design. Hems are delicately edged with picot using the lace carriage, but this can easily be achieved manually if you haven't got a lace carriage.

SILK·BLOUSE

Here the basic shape of the sweater has been slightly altered to give a wider neckline and a shaped sleeve for a summer blouse knitted in a fine blend of silk and cotton. The rolled edge detail is simple and easy, and gives a delicate lightweight finish, complementing the delicacy of the yarn. Designed to be long and loose, but coming in close and low on the hip, the style is easily altered to a shorter version.

· Angora sweater ·

Yarn: Celandine Amanda, 50% chinchilla, 50% lambswool, 4 ply equivalent. 1 cone (340gm/12oz). Sweater uses 320gm/11oz
Machine: Standard
Tension: MT6, giving 32sts, 44rs to a 10cm/4in square. Hems T4. Remember to wash your tension square before measuring
Measurements: Length 62cm/25in; chest 100cm/40in. Adjust as required. Follow the diagram for stitches and rows

FRONT

Bottom hem: Cast on WY and K several rs, ending with carr at R
Using MY, K 1r T9
K 20rs T4
K 1r T7
Carr at R
Transfer sts for picot. If using lace carriage, where Ns are selected, move it across the Ns from L to R. All Ns are selected. Using 1×1 pusher, push EON back to WP. Move lace carriage across Ns to L. The sts will be transferred. Continue knitting with main carriage. Otherwise insert a card locking on a row with EON punched out, and follow your machine's instruction for lace.
K 20rs T4
K 1r T9
Carr at L
To turn up the hem: K 1r T10
Carr at R, MT6
Follow diagram
At armholes: Cast off 16sts at beginning of rs161 and 162

At front neck: Bring all Ns to L of 0 out to HP, and 8 to R of 0, K 1r. Either wrap the yarn around N8, or use automatic wrapping technique as described in Chapter 6.
K back to R
Continue to shape, bringing out 4sts at neck edge every 2rs twice, 3sts every 2rs 4 times, and 2 sts every 2rs 4 times. 28sts remain
Break MY, join in WY and knit several rows, ending carr at R. Break yarn.
Carr still on hold, move to L of machine; sts on WY will drop. Tuck this part of the knitting round the back of work and secure with a weight.
Now replace Ns at L to UWP, except for 8 to L of 0.
Finish L side as for R, ending with several rs WY. Break yarn.
Carr still on hold, move to R of machine; sts on WY will drop. Secure with a weight as before. The sts for the neck will remain at HP.
Neckband: Set carriage to K sts back to WP
Push up 1N extra at either end of sts. 74sts
K 1r T9
K 6rs T4
K 1r T7
Carr at R. Work picot as before
K 6rs T4
1r T9
Carr at L
Turn up, picking up the sts on the first loose row (T9) onto the corresponding Ns
K 1r T10
Cast off with the latch tool

BACK

The pattern details for the back are the same as the front, except that the back neck shaping begins at RC 246. The carr is set to hold, all the sts to the L of 0, and 16 to the R are brought to HP.
K 2rs
Carr at R
Bring 4sts to HP at neck edge 5 times every 2rs
Finish as for front
To join the shoulders on the machine: With right side of one piece of work facing pick up one set of shoulder sts onto the Ns
With wrong side of the other piece of work facing, pick up the matching shoulder sts onto the corresponding Ns
K 1r T10
Cast off with the latch tool
Join the other shoulder to match

SLEEVES (both alike)

Push up 144 Ns, 72 to L and 72 to R of 0
With the wrong side facing hook up 1st either side of the shoulder seam at armhole edge either side of centre 0
Hook up a st at the bottom of the armhole onto N72 at L, and at N72 at R
Pick up evenly along the armhole edge
Try to pick up along the same line of sts
Knit sleeve according to diagram
A 'finishing' hem: K 1r T9
K 10rs T4
K 1r T7
Work picot
K 10rs T4
K 1r T9
Turn up, picking up sts on first loose row (T9) onto corresponding Ns
K 1r T10
Cast off with the latch tool

MAKING UP

Finish off any insecure ends, leaving only those which may be used for sewing up. Wash garment, pressing when almost dry. Backstitch seams, slip stitch hems at neck and edges. Press seams.

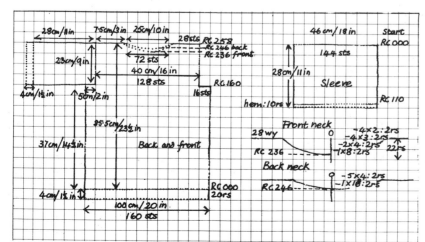

· Silk blouse ·

Yarn: Celandine Sienna, 50% silk, 30% cotton, 20% acrylic, 2 ply equivalent. 1 cone (250gm/9oz) each main colour and contrast. Blouse uses approximately 150gm/5oz MY and 120gm/4oz contrast

Machine: Standard

Pattern cards: Jones card 15G for main garment, Knitmaster card 2 for the hems

Tension: MT5, giving 34sts, 40rs to a 10cm/4in square

Measurements: Length 62cm/25in; chest 100cm/40in. Follow the diagram for stitches and rows

FRONT

No hem is knitted until one side is finished, when the stitches at the bottom are picked up in such a way as to slightly gather the work.

Cast on in WY, ending with carr at L

Insert main pattern card and lock on r1

With MY in feeder 1, K 1r MT, setting pattern

RC 000

Release card

Contrast yarn in feeder 2, carr set for FI, continue knitting

At armholes:

Mark at RC 130 to facilitate picking up the sleeve sts

At front neck:

Stop at RC 210, make a note of the card row number

Put R shoulder sts on WY

Replace Ns at L to WP manually, reset pattern card and lock

With carr set to hold and slip, and to set the pattern, move it to the L of work. Shape L side to correspond with R and leave shoulder sts on WY

Neckband: Carr at L

Insert pattern card for hem, lock on r1

With MY in feeder and carriage set for stockinet K 1r MT, setting pattern

Release card, contrast yarn in feeder 2 carr set for FI.

K 6rs T1 FI

Remove both yarns from feeders. Break off MY

Replace contrast in feeder 1. Set carr for stockinet

K 6rs T1

K 5rs T5

K 1r T10, carr at R

Cast off with the latch tool

Bottom hem: Insert card 2, lock on R1. Push up 128Ns to WP, carr at L

With wrong side of work facing, pick up from WY at the bottom of the work

Starting from R, put 1st on each of the first and second Ns at R, ie N64 and N63, 2sts on the third N (N62), 1st on each of fourth and fifth N, 2sts on sixth and so on

Do not pull Ns out to HP, leave them at WP

Set carr to slip and set pattern to R RC 000. Release card, contrast in feeder 1, MY in feeder 2, carr set for FI

K 20rs T1 FI, carr at R

Set carr for stockinet, remove MY from feeder 2

K 12rs T1

K 9rs T5

K 1r T10, carr at R. Cast off with the latch tool

BACK

Work as for front to RC 220, shaping neck according to diagram Join back to front at shoulders on machine, right sides together, knitting across all sts on T10 before casting off with the latch tool.

SLEEVES (both alike)

Push up 170Ns to WP

Wrong side of work facing, shoulder seam at centre 0, markers at N85 L and N85 R of 0, pick up 170sts evenly along armhole edge

Carr at L. Lock card on r1. MY in feeder 1, K 1r T5 stockinet, setting pattern

Carr at R. Set for FI. Contrast in feeder 2, RC 000

K as diagram ending RC 80, carr at R

Change to card 2, lock on r1

Remove yarns from feeders. Make sure all Ns are at WP. If selected, push back to WP

Set carr to slip but not to pattern, move carr to L, set pattern as you return to R

Replace contrast in main feeder, MY in feeder 2

Release card, set carr for FI

K 12rs T1 FI Break off MY. Contrast in main feeder

K 8rs T1 stockinet

K 5rs T5

K 1r T10, carr at R. Cast off with the latch tool.

MAKING UP

Press garment with a cool iron. Back stitch all seams and darn in ends. Press seams. Allow hems at neck sleeve and bottom edges to 'roll' naturally.

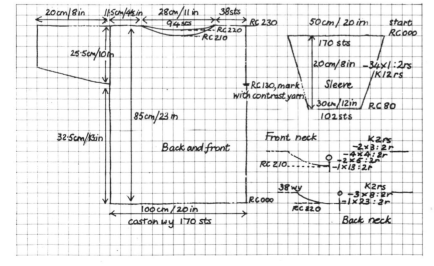

SWEATER · IN · SLUB · COTTON

This summer sweater, knitted on the chunky machine, is shown here in tuck stitch pattern, the 'purl' side being the right side. The yarn itself gives a lovely surface texture and the sweater looks equally pretty simply in reverse stocking stitch. The effect of the tuck pattern is to further enhance the texture, and combined with a slightly looser tension than usual gives a lacy, casual summer garment.

Knitted in one with the main garment, the sleeves are slightly gathered onto a reverse stocking stitch cuff. Keep your eye on the needles as you knit, sometimes the 'slub' catches in the hooks when tucking. And move your weights 'out' as you shape. This is a good initiation to using tuck stitch as the irregularity of the yarn covers up the odd mistake!

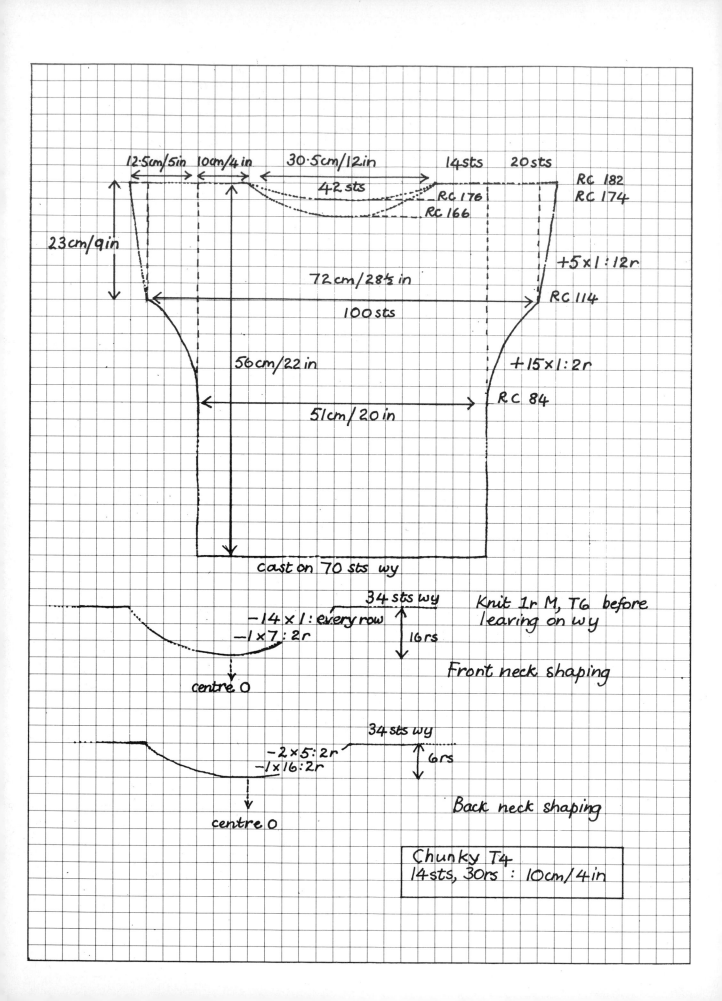

12.5cm/5in   10cm/4in   30.5cm/12in   14sts   20sts

42 sts

RC 182
RC 174

RC 176
RC 166

23cm/9in

+5×1:12r

72cm/28½ in

RC 114

100 sts

56cm/22 in

+15×1:2r

RC 84

51cm/20 in

cast on 70 sts wy

34 sts wy

−14×1: every row

−1×7:2r

16rs

Knit 1r M, T6 before
leaving on wy

centre 0

Front neck shaping

34 sts wy

−2×5:2r

−1×16:2r

6rs

centre 0

Back neck shaping

Chunky T4
14sts, 30rs : 10cm/4in

Yarn: Atkinson's slub cotton. 1 cone (350gm/12oz). Sweater uses 315gm/11oz

Machine: Chunky

Pattern card: Jones/Brother 7p from main set, or any tuck stitch card

Tension: MT 4, giving 30rs, 14sts to a 10cm/4in square

Measurements: Length 61cm/24in; bust 112cm/44in

FRONT and BACK

Bottom hems: Cast on in WY, K several rs ending carr at R

With MY:

K 1r T4

K 18rs T0

K 1r T4

K 18rs T0

K 1r T4

Remove MY but do not break off

Knit several rs WY, release from the machine

Carr at L

Turn work, having smooth side of work facing, and MY at L. Replace sts onto Ns, turn up hem

Insert card. Lock on r1

K 1r T6, setting pattern. Carr at R

Fit tuck brushes if used

Follow diagram. Remember to make a note of card row number at RC 166 front, 176 back. Knit to RC 182 at R shoulder, carr at R.

K 1r T8 MY. Break off MY and put sts onto WY

Finish left shoulder to match, taking care to replace Ns at HP to WP before setting pattern

Neckband: With carr at R, set for stockinet, K sts at HP:

* K 1r T4 K 6rs T0 K 1r T4 K 6rs T0 1K 1r T4

Do not break MY, remove from feeder

K several rs WY, release from machine

Turn work. Carr and yarn at R

Replace sts on Ns, turn up the hem:

Pick up on loose row

K 2rs T10, cast off with the latch tool*

Shoulders: Carr at R

With the purl side of one section facing you, pick up one set of shoulder sts

With the smooth side of the other section facing you, pick up corresponding shoulder sts

K 2rs T10

Cast off with the latch tool

Sleeve bands: Carr at R

Push 46Ns to WP

Hang the sleeve edge onto machine, purl side of work facing, shoulder seam at centre 0. Underarm seams on N23 L and R. Pick up evenly, putting 2 loops onto a needle where necessary, to gather edge

Knit hem as for neck band from * to *

MAKING UP

Finish off ends. Back stitch seams and slip stitch hems. Press lightly if wished – the sweater in the photograph was left unpressed to maintain its 'cellular' quality.

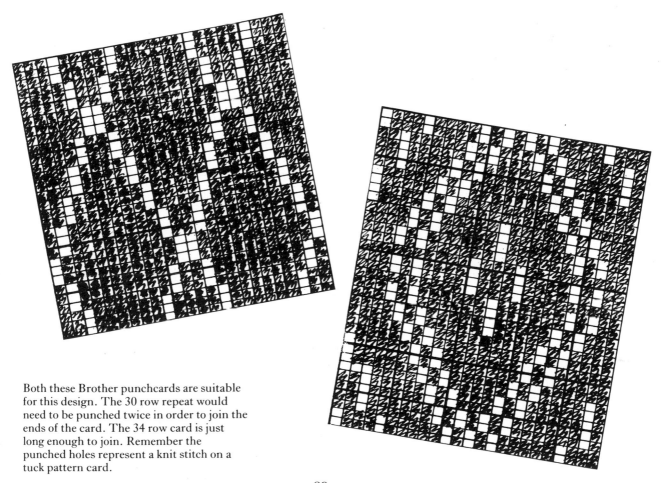

Both these Brother punchcards are suitable for this design. The 30 row repeat would need to be punched twice in order to join the ends of the card. The 34 row card is just long enough to join. Remember the punched holes represent a knit stitch on a tuck pattern card.

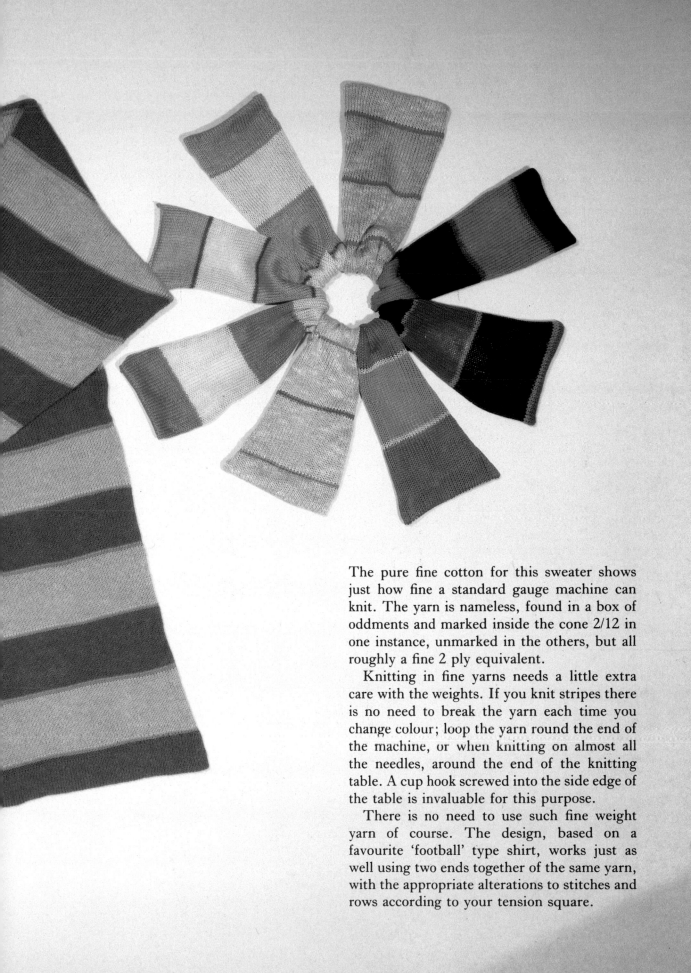

The pure fine cotton for this sweater shows just how fine a standard gauge machine can knit. The yarn is nameless, found in a box of oddments and marked inside the cone 2/12 in one instance, unmarked in the others, but all roughly a fine 2 ply equivalent.

Knitting in fine yarns needs a little extra care with the weights. If you knit stripes there is no need to break the yarn each time you change colour; loop the yarn round the end of the machine, or when knitting on almost all the needles, around the end of the knitting table. A cup hook screwed into the side edge of the table is invaluable for this purpose.

There is no need to use such fine weight yarn of course. The design, based on a favourite 'football' type shirt, works just as well using two ends together of the same yarn, with the appropriate alterations to stitches and rows according to your tension square.

Yarn: 2/12 cotton, 2 ply equivalent. 120gm/4oz Col 1, 100gm/3½oz Col 2, 30gm/1oz Col 3
Also required: 3×100mm/⅜in buttons
Machine: Standard
Tension: MT1, giving 38sts, 60rs to 10cm/4in
Measurements: Length 64cm/25in, chest 102cm/40in
Hems are on T0, loose rows on T2, turn up rows on T4. Decide which colour you want to use for the hems and bands and call it Col 1, the second colour, is Col 2, and the fine line of colour between them is Col 3.

FRONT

Bottom hem: Cast on WY
K several rs ending carr at R
Using Col 1, K 1r T2, 20rs T0, 1r T2, 20rs T0, 1r T2
Turn up the hem, and K 1r T4.
Carr at R, change to MT1
K 2rs Col 3
K 30rs Col 2
K 2rs Col 3
K 30rs Col 1
This is the colour sequence throughout. Follow the diagram for stitches and rows. Change colour at the R, and hang a weight at R edge to prevent the strands of yarn tightening as you take them up the side of the work
Mark the underarm with contrast yarn to facilitate picking up the armhole sts.
Dividing for front opening:
Make a note of the row number of the stripe
Finish the R side first, all sts at L of 0, and 5 to R of 0 at HP. As you knit, weight the work at the centre carefully and keep moving your weights up. You will need to hand wrap or automatically wrap the Ns for the neck shaping to avoid holes
After shaping neck, at RC 360, knit across all shoulder sts on T2. Finish with several rs WY. Release from machine.
Push the 29 neckline sts at R back to UWP
K 1r Col 1 T2
Break yarn, K several rs WY. Release from machine
With a length of yarn, cast off

centre 10sts loosely
Move carr to L. Reset RC, set carriage to K back from HP
Finish L side to match R side, remembering to K 1r Col 1, T2 across neckline sts before finishing on WY

BACK

Work from diagram to RC 340, either hand wrap or automatically wrap the yarn when shaping the neck
Remember to work 1r T2 Col 1 before putting shoulders and neck onto WY

FRONT OPENING BANDS

Left band: With wrong side of front facing pick up 35sts evenly from the left side of the front opening
K 1r T2
K 20rs T0
K 1r T2
K 20rs T0
K 1r T2
Turn up the hem picking up on the first loose row
K 1r T4
Cast off with the latch tool
Right band: With wrong side facing pick up 35sts evenly from R side of the front opening
K 1r T2
K 10rs T0
Buttonholes: Working from the left, transfer 12th st from L onto N11, 13th st onto N14, 24th st onto N23, 25th st onto N26
Leave empty Ns at WP, K 1r
With transfer tool, 'e' wrap the strand of yarn on the buttonhole needles. This is easier to control if you bring the needles at either side to HP.
Bring the buttonhole Ns out to HP after 'e' wrapping to facilitate knitting on r11
K 9rs T0
K 1r T2
K 10rs T0
Work buttonholes on rs10 and 11 as before
K 9rs T0
K 1r T2
Turn up a hem as for L front
Join right shoulder: With right sides of work together, and wrong

side of front of garment facing you, pick up the shoulder sts, back sts first, then front sts
K across all sts on T4
Cast off with the latch tool
Neckband (two sections): Push up 113Ns to WP
With wrong side of work facing, pick up the section of the neckline which includes the shoulder you have just joined in this way:
Starting at L, pick up 10sts from the top edge of front band, leaving the facing free. Pick up 29sts from the front neck, 4sts from the space at the shoulder edge, 68sts from the back neck and 2sts from the space at the shoulder (113sts)
K 10rs T0
Work buttonhole, transferring sixth st from L onto N5 and seventh st onto N8, 'e' wrapping on 11th r as before
Finish as for front bands, matching buttonhole on N6 and N7
For second section push up 41Ns
Starting at L, pick up 2sts from the space between the shoulder sts and neckline sts, 29sts from front neckline, 10sts from the top edge of the front band, leaving the facing free. 41sts.
K a 20r hem to match the first neckband section
Join left shoulder

SLEEVES

Follow diagram, working a 20r hem to start with, following the colour sequence as for the front
Work the last row on T2
Work several rs of WY. Release from the machine.
Joining sleeves to armholes: Push up 190Ns
With right side of sleeve facing, replace stitches onto machine
With wrong side of garment facing pick up at armhole edge, centring shoulder seam at 0, and armhole markers at Ns95 at L and R
It may be necessary to cut the yarns which were carried up the sides of front and back if they restrict the stretch of the garment. Do this evenly, so that they can be darned in afterwards
K 1r T4
Cast off with the latch tool

MAKING UP

Slip stitch neckband facing at front to the seam and mattress stitch join at L shoulder. Slip stitch bottom of front band to 10 cast off stitches at bottom of opening, button band first, buttonhole section over the top. Leave the facing edge of the buttonhole band free to reduce bulk at this point. Oversew neatly around the buttonhole edges.

Press carefully on the wrong side of garment. The hems and neckbands are best steamed, holding the iron just above the fabric. Sew the side and underarm seams, matching the stripes, and press flat. Sew on the buttons.

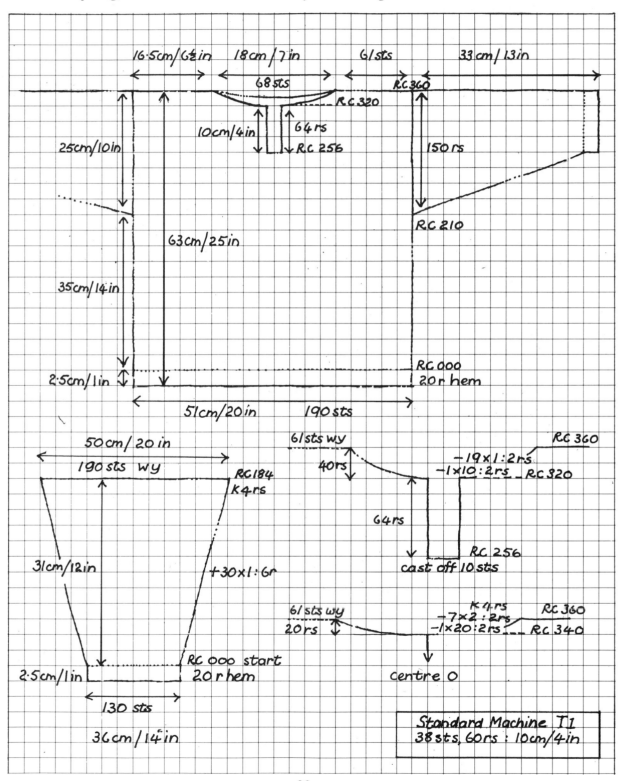

TWEED·JACKETS

Check position of R.1 on your machine.
Tweed punchcard. 10r repeat.

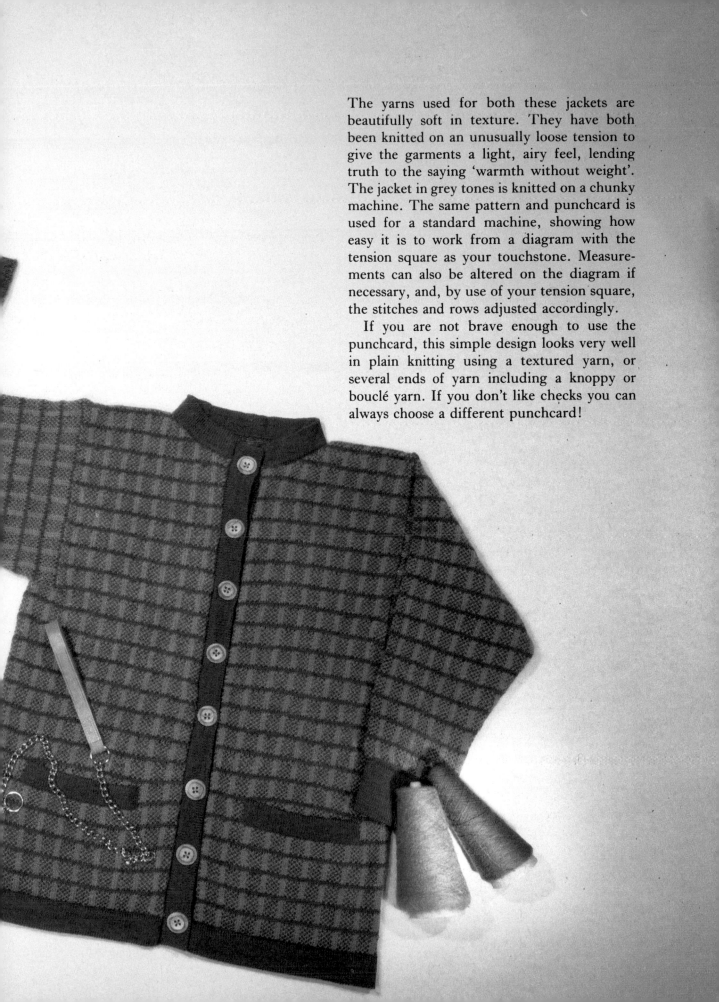

The yarns used for both these jackets are beautifully soft in texture. They have both been knitted on an unusually loose tension to give the garments a light, airy feel, lending truth to the saying 'warmth without weight'. The jacket in grey tones is knitted on a chunky machine. The same pattern and punchcard is used for a standard machine, showing how easy it is to work from a diagram with the tension square as your touchstone. Measurements can also be altered on the diagram if necessary, and, by use of your tension square, the stitches and rows adjusted accordingly.

If you are not brave enough to use the punchcard, this simple design looks very well in plain knitting using a textured yarn, or several ends of yarn including a knoppy or bouclé yarn. If you don't like checks you can always choose a different punchcard!

· Chunky jacket ·

Yarn: Atkinson's Rhapsody, 18% wool, 67% acrylic, 15% nylon. 1 cone (500gm/17½oz). Atkinson's Fantasia, 11% wool, 71% acrylic, 18% polyester. 1 cone (500gm/17½oz) Jacket uses 340gm/12oz Rhapsody, 240gm/8½oz Fantasia.

Also required: 7×28mm/1⅛in buttons and shoulder pads (optional)

Pattern card: Your choice, or punch according to diagram given for tweed punchcard

Tension: T8, giving 16sts and 18rs to a 10cm/4in square

Measurements: Length 76cm/30in, underarm 126cm/50in

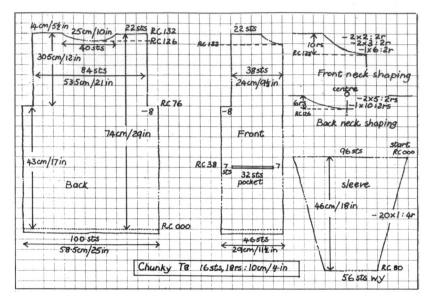

NOTES FOR CHUNKY MACHINES

Whenever you knit a row on a tight tension after a loose row, check that all the stitches have knitted properly. If not, a pull at the work will generally solve the problem. If you are using the tweed punchcard, it is a ten row repeat, of which the ninth and tenth rows are unpatterned. If your machine selects the end needles of these rows, push them back, or the stitches will drop. It is not always necessary to remove the contrast colour from feeder 2 on these rows, but knit them carefully in case the second colour catches in the brushes.

BANDS

All bands except for those at the top of the pocket are knitted as follows:
K 1r T8
K 14rs T0
K 1r T8
K 14rs T0
K 1r T8
Turn up and K 1r T10
The pocket bands are the same tensions, but are 10 rows deep as opposed to 14 rows. The cuffs are 24 rows deep.

BACK

Insert card. Lock on r1. Push up 100Ns to WP. Follow diagram, leaving shoulders on waste yarn, bringing up an extra needle at either end of the neckline stitches before knitting the neckband.

LEFT FRONT

Insert card. Lock on r1. Push up 46Ns to WP
Cast on in WY and K several rs, ending carr at L
Join in MY. Knit and turn up hem, setting pattern on last row
Carr at L
RC 000, MT8
Join in contrast yarn
K FI to RC 38. Lock card on r9.
Set carr to hold
To knit pocket: Bring 7Ns at L, 7 at R to HP. Break yarns
Knitting on 32 pocket sts, K pocket hem in MY, stockinet
Knit pocket pouch:
K 34rs T7
K 1r T10 setting pattern
RC 000. Release card, join in contrast, and K FI T8 to RC 30. Carr at R
Break yarns. Replace all Ns to WP
Set carr to slip moving to L over all sts setting pattern. Reset RC to 38. Release card
Continue to RC 76, casting off 8sts for armhole at beginning of row
At RC 122, shape neck according to diagram, leave 22 shoulder sts on WY
Bring up 1 extra N at L of neckline sts before knitting the neckband

RIGHT FRONT

Insert card, lock on r1. Push up 46Ns to WP
Knit to match L front, reversing shapings by reading L for R and R for L

FRONT BANDS

Left band: Push up 114Ns to WP
Fold front in half to find centre of front edge. Place at centre of machine
Hook up bottom edge at N57 L and top of neckband at N57 R. Don't catch in the facings
Pick up evenly along front edge of garment and knit a band, casting off with the latch tool.

Right band: Work buttonholes as follows:
Set RC after first loose row
Pick up as for L band, working to RC 7
Select buttonhole Ns as follows:
Starting at the 11th N from the end of the work, K Ns 11, 12, 13 and 14 by hand with contrast yarn. Continue thus across all sts, so that the buttonholes are set in groups of 4sts, with 11sts between each one, and 10sts at either end of the machine. Continue to knit the band, working the buttonholes on the seventh row of the facing, either finishing them on the machine, or knitting them again by hand for finishing later (see section on buttonholes in Chapter 6)
The buttonholes on the photographed jacket were worked on the machine

SLEEVES

Join shoulders on machine

Pick up 96sts at armhole edge. Follow diagram, leave sts on WY at cuff

Push up 42Ns, replace cuff sts, putting 2sts on every third N

Knit cuff, casting off with the latch tool

MAKING UP

Slip stitch hems together at open edges, and bottom hems to front facings. Slip stitch pocket hems to fronts of garment and pocket edges together. Back-stitch underarm and sleeve seams. Mattress stitch seams at cuffs and neckband. Sew on buttons to correspond with buttonholes.

· Standard jacket ·

Yarn: Celadine Sara; 70% acrylic, 20% wool, 10% alpaca, 1 cone (350gm/12½oz). Celadine Dawn, 70% super kid mohair, 30% nylon, 1 cone (245gm/8½oz). Two ends of mohair are used together; wind off approximately 100gm/13½oz into a separate ball Jacket uses 300gm/11oz Sara, 150gm/6oz Dawn

Also required: 8×28mm/1⅛in buttons and shoulder pads (optional)

Pattern card: Your choice, or punch according to diagram given for tweed punchcard

Tension: T9, giving 29sts and 32rs to a 10cm/4in square

Measurements: Length 76cm/30in, underarm 126cm/50in

The method of working is the same as for the chunky jacket. Refer to the diagram for rows and stitches and to the notes below for different details.

BANDS

All bands except for the top of the pocket are as follows:

K 1r T8
K 20rs T3
K 1r T8
K 20rs T3
K 1r T8

Turn up, and K 1r T10

The pocket bands are 16rs deep, the cuffs are 40rs long

POCKETS

After working pocket hem in MY stockinet, knit pocket pouch

With MY K 56rs T6 for pocket facing

K 1r T10, setting pattern on r1 of card

Release card

K 48rs M'1'8, FI

Lock card on r49, replace all Ns to WP and reset pattern

Reset RC to 48, release card, continue knitting

FRONT BANDS

Left band: Push 200Ns to WP (see notes for chunky jacket)

Right band: Work as for L band to RC 10

Select buttonhole Ns as follows: Starting at 11th N from the end of the work, K Ns11, 12, 13, 14, 15 by hand with contrast yarn. Continue thus across all sts, so that the buttonholes are set in groups of 5sts, with 20sts between each one, and 10sts at either end of the machine. Continue to knit the band, working the buttonholes on r10 of the facing, either finishing them on the machine, or knitting them again by hand (see section on buttonholes in Chapter 6).

SLEEVES

Join shoulders on machine

Pick up 174sts at armhole edge. Follow diagram, leaving sts on WY at cuffs

Use 3×1 transfer tool for fully-fashioned shaping, transferring the second and third st from each end to the 4th and 5th N. Push the 2 empty Ns back to NWP

Push up 77Ns, replace cuff sts putting 2sts on every third N.

Knit cuff, casting off with latch tool

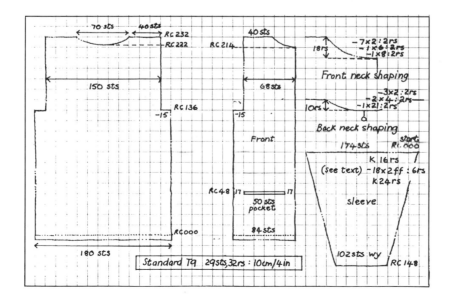

97

MOHAIR · MIX · SWEATER

Quickly and simply knitted, this is a very good beginner's sweater. The yarn used for the garment illustrated flows through the chunky machine like a dream, producing an interesting fabric with a light surface texture – the colour is reminiscent of crushed raspberries. Fashion details are the bands, set on sideways, and the collar being caught down at the front with a simulated knot.

As far as possible everything is joined on the machine, however here is a great chance to practise grafting. All the bands have been joined in this way, the large stitch making it easy and quick to work. If you have never grafted before it is well worth trying it on this sweater, but if you don't feel confident enough, the band ends can of course be joined on the machine, and alternative instructions are given for this.

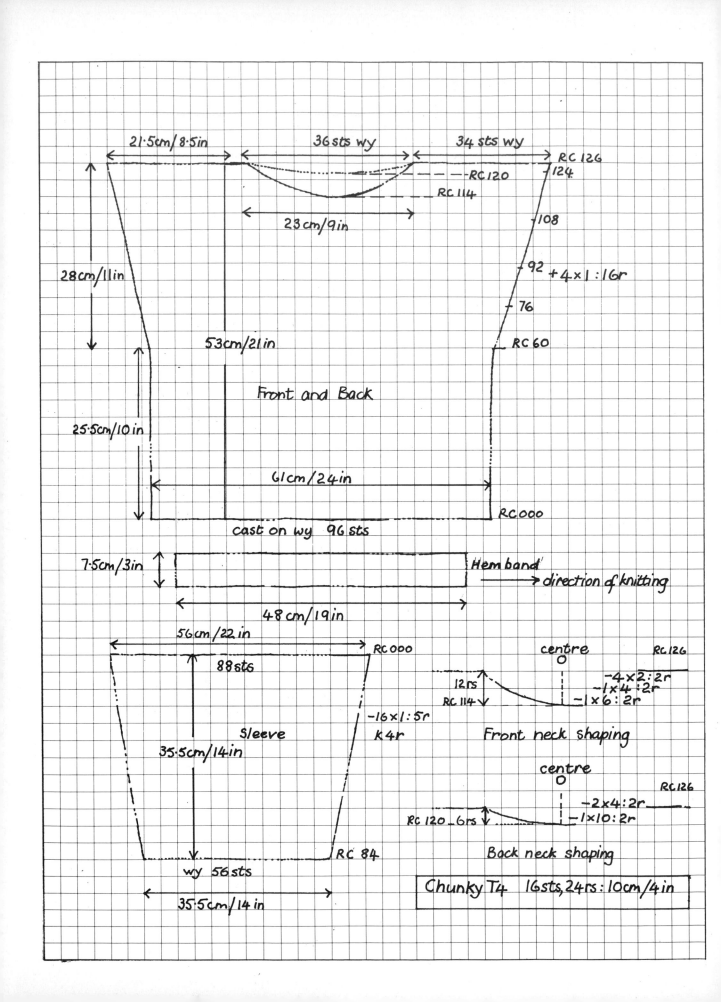

21.5cm/8.5in   36 sts wy   34 sts wy

RC 126
RC 120 — 124
RC 114

23cm/9in

28cm/11in

108

92 +4×1:16r

76

RC 60

53cm/21in

Front and Back

25.5cm/10in

61cm/24in

RC 000

cast on wy 96 sts

7.5cm/3in   Hem band
→ direction of knitting

48cm/19in

56cm/22in   RC 000

88 sts

12 rs
RC 114

centre ○   RC 126
−4×2:2r
−1×4:2r
−1×6:2r

−16×1:5r
k4r

Sleeve   Front neck shaping

35.5cm/14in

centre ○   RC 126
−2×4:2r
RC 120 6rs −1×10:2r

RC 84

Back neck shaping

wy 56 sts

35.5cm/14in

Chunky T4   16 sts, 24 rs : 10cm/4in

Yarn: Atkinson's Fantasia, 11% wool, 71% acrylic, 18% polyester. 1 cone (500gm/17½oz). Sweater uses 480gm/17oz. It is best to purchase an extra 100gm/3½oz (balled) for extra needs

Machine: Chunky

Tension: MT4, giving 16sts and 24rs to a 10cm/4in square

Measurements: A loose fitting sweater, length 61cm/24in, chest 122cm/48in. Follow the diagrams for stitches and rows

The hems, bands in this instance, are knitted separately and joined onto the body afterwards.

FRONT

Cast on WY and K several rs ending carr at R

RC 000 K 1r T6, continue on MT, marking bottom of armhole with contrast yarn

Leave shoulder sts on WY

Before leaving neckline sts on WY, K 1r T6 in MY (36sts)

BACK

Work as for front, following diagram for back neck shaping, and knitting 1r T6 on the neckline sts before leaving on WY (36sts)

COLLAR

Cast on 36sts WY, K several rs ending carr at R

With MY, K 100rs. Leave on WY

Join one shoulder on machine: Push up 34Ns to WP

With right side of front facing, pick up shoulder sts onto Ns

With wrong side of back facing, pick up matching shoulder sts onto corresponding Ns

K across all sts T8

Cast off with the latch tool

Join collar to neck: Push up 80Ns to WP

With right side of collar facing, hook up 80sts evenly from one long edge

With right side of the garment facing replace neckline sts onto the machine thus:

Pick up 2 extra sts from space between neckline sts and shoulder sts on WY at either end, and 4 extra sts at the centre, in the space between the neckline sts at the shoulder-join (80sts in all)

K 2rs T8

Cast off with the latch tool

Join the second shoulder on the machine

If you are not grafting, join the ends of the collar now, on the machine

SLEEVES

Push up 88Ns to WP

With wrong side of garment facing, pick up 88sts evenly from armhole edge, centring shoulder seam at 0, coloured markers at N44 on either side

Follow the diagram for the sleeve, working r84 on T6 before leaving on WY (56sts)

Sleeve bands (knit 2): Push up 37Ns to WP, 18 to L and 19 to R of 0. Push N1 at R of 0 to NWP

K several rs WY

Using MY, K 60rs T2

Finish with several rs WY, release from machine

Join bands to sleeves: Push up 35Ns to WP, 17 to L of 0, 18 to R of 0

With right side of sleeve facing, and starting from R, pick up sts from WY as follows:

Put 2sts on N18, 1st on N17, and so on to N5 (1st on N5)

Put 2sts on each of the next 7Ns, then 1st on N4 at L, 2sts on N5, and so on, ending with 2sts on N17 at L

With wrong side of band facing, pick up 35sts evenly from one long edge onto corresponding Ns. (If you are not grafting cast off now: K 1r T8, cast off with the latch tool, join cuff ends on the machine)

Fold cuff, and pick up along the other edge in the same manner. Bring all Ns out to HP to facilitate knitting. K carefully across all sts, T8

Cast off with the latch tool

Bottom bands (knit 2): Work as for sleeve bands, but K 120rs

To join bands to garment: Push up 72Ns to WP

With right side of front facing, and starting from R, pick up sts from WY at the bottom of the garment as follows:

Put 1st on each of N36 and N35, 2sts on N34. Continue like this, putting 2sts on every third N to end

With wrong side of band facing, pick up 72sts evenly along one long edge, onto corresponding Ns. (If you are not grafting, cast off now: K 1r T8, cast off with latch tool)

Fold band and pick up along the other edge in the same manner

Finish as for sleeve bands

MAKING UP

Graft the ends of the bands together, from the right side in the case of sleeve and waist bands, since these form a tube. Check that your stitch is forming correctly – the tendency is to produce a 'purl' row on the right side. If you have joined the ends on the machine, fold waistband, and slip stitch to bottom of sweater. Fold cuffs and slip stitch to bottom of sleeve. Back stitch all seams. Press the seams lightly with a cool dry iron.

KNOT (optional)

Cast on 30sts by hand

K 36rs T2

Cast off with the latch tool

To attach knot: Make three vertical pleats, and attach to centre from neckline on the seam, taking the pleated strip over the collar, and attaching it to correspond on the inside.

SILK·JACKET

The least expensive of all the silk yarns, the silk noil used for this jacket is naturally and lightly textured. The little flecks are the remains of the cocoon from which the high grade silk was spun. Silk absorbs colour in its own special way, giving a matt brilliance to all the colours in the range, however delicate.

Tension 8 on a standard machine gives a firm fabric, suitable for a jacket. If you plan to use noil silk for a sweater, tension 9 or 10 will give softer results. You can still take the tension down as far as 4 for hems if you need to.

The fashion details on the jacket are achieved by basic machine techniques, fully explained in the instructions. The construction shows how versatile a machine can be when it comes to organising shapes. Everything is possible with holding position and waste yarn. The sleeve shaping is fully fashioned which, apart from looking good, is a much quicker technique than simple decreasing.

Yarn: Texere Silk Noil. 2 cones (350gm/12oz each). Jacket uses 500gm/17½oz

Also required: 1×28mm/1⅛in button, shoulder pads (optional) and medium weight iron-on vilene (optional)

Machine: Standard.

Tension: MT8, giving 28sts and 38rs to a 10cm/4in square

Measurements: Length 51cm/20in, chest 122cm/48in, width at bottom of jacket 100cm/40in. This is a roomy style for all sizes. Follow diagrams for stitches and rows

Silk noil hangs lightly in the needles, so watch the weights as you knit, particularly the pockets.

BACK

Cast on WY ending carr at R
Join in MY
K 1r T10
K 20rs T5
K 1r T10
RC 000 (shape following diagram)
K 20rs T5
K 1r T10. Do not turn up the hem
Change to MT8 and continue, marking bottom of armholes at RC 76 with contrast yarn
After neckline shaping is finished, and both shoulders are on WY, finish the neckband as follows:
Bring out 1 extra N either end of the neckline (46sts)
K 1r T10
K 12rs T5
K 1r T10
K 12rs T5
K 1r T10, break yarn
Leave sts on several rs WY

LEFT FRONT

Cast on WY 70sts, K several rs, carr at R
K 1r T10
K 20rs T5
K 1r T10, carr at R
Bring out 15Ns at R to HP
Push back N36 at R to NWP, and leave at NWP throughout knitting
Cast on 14sts ('e' wrap)
RC 000, follow diagram for shaping (bring cast-on sts to hold, and K back to WP until you can hang a weight)
K 20rs T5

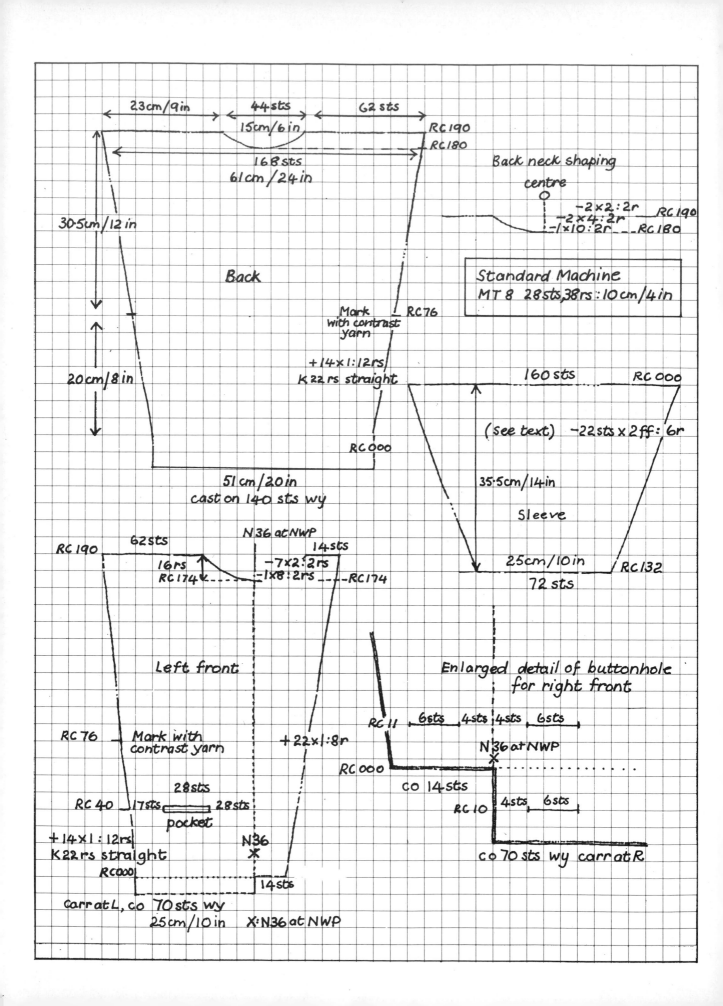

Back

23cm/9in 44 sts 62 sts

15cm/6in

168 sts

61cm/24in

RC 190
RC 180

30·5cm/12 in

20cm/8in

Mark with contrast yarn RC 76

+14×1:12rs
K 22 rs straight

RC 000

51 cm/20 in
cast on 140 sts wy

Back neck shaping
centre

−2×2:2r RC 190
−2×4:2r
−1×10:2r RC 180

Standard Machine
MT 8 28 sts, 38 rs : 10 cm/4 in

160 sts RC 000

(see text) −22 sts × 2 ff : 6r

35·5cm/14in

Sleeve

25cm/10in RC 132
72 sts

Left front

RC 190 62 sts N 36 at NWP 14 sts

16 rs −7×2:2rs
RC 174 −1×8:2rs RC 174

RC 76 Mark with contrast yarn

+22×1:8r

RC 40 17sts 28 sts 28 sts
pocket

+14×1:12rs
K 22 rs straight

RC 000

N 36
×

14 sts

Carr at L, co 70 sts wy
25cm/10in X:N36 at NWP

Enlarged detail of buttonhole
for right front

RC 11 6sts 4sts 4sts 6sts

N 36 at NWP
×

RC 000 co 14 sts

RC 10 4sts 6sts

co 70 sts wy carr at R

K 1r T10
Continue MT8 to RC 40, carr at R, break yarn
Set carr to hold
Bring out all Ns to HP, except for 28sts for pocket (see diagram)
Join in yarn
Knit pocket hem:
K 1r T10
K 10rs T5
K 1r T10
K 10rs T5
K 1r T10
Turn up pocket hem
Hang weight behind work if sts tend to rise out of Ns
Pick up every other st on the loose row and put onto the corresponding N, it makes the next row easier to knit
K 1r T10
Pocket pouch: K 30rs T6
K 1r T10
K 30rs T6, carr at L
Break yarn
Set carr to slip and hold, move to R of machine. Set carr to knit
Reset RC to 40, MT8. Carry on knitting, increasing as in diagram, marking armhole at RC 76, to RC 174, carr at R
Set carr to hold
N36 at NWP is centre front
Shape R side first, using holding position, according to diagram
Leave 14sts at R on WY
Carr still on hold. Move across to L of work, 14sts on WY drop from Ns
Replace those Ns to NWP.
Finish L side: Push all Ns at L of 0, and 27 to R of 0 to UWP (28 if you are wrapping automatically)
Shape L side according to diagram.
Leave 62 shoulder sts on WY
Carr still on hold, move to R
All neck sts are now on hold.
Push 22Ns at R of centre front (N36 at NWP) to UWP
K 1r MT8, MY
Break MY, K several rs WY, release from machine
Replace 22Ns at L of centre front to WP with eyelet tool
Fold lapel facing at centre, and hook up 22sts of facing onto the 22Ns at L of centre front
Cast off 5 at R loosely (hang weight on edge stitch). Use length of MY

which remains at centre front for this
Bring up extra N at L (18sts)
Join in MY
K 1r T10
K 12rs T5
K 1r T10
K 12rs T5
K 1r T10
Break MY
Finish on several rs WY. Release from machine

RIGHT FRONT

Work as for left front, starting with carr at L, reading L for R, and R for L, reversing all shapings. *In addition*, work buttonhole in hem and front facing thus:
Bottom hem: Cast on WY 70sts, K several rs
Carr at L, RC 000
K 1r T10
K 9rs T5
Counting from L of machine, knit Ns5, 6, 7, 8, 9 and 10 by hand in contrast yarn for buttonhole
K 11rs T5
K 1r T10
Bring out 15sts at L to HP, pushing back N36 at L to NWP as for L front
Cast on by hand as before
RC 000 (follow diagram for shaping)
K 11rs T5
Counting from N36 at NWP (centre front) K Ns5, 6, 7, 8, 9 and 10 to L and R of centre front in contrast yarn
K 9rs T5
K 1r T10
Carry on in MT8 to RC 40
Work pocket
Mark armhole at RC 76
Shape at RC 174 as for L front, starting carr at L
Join fronts to back on the machine at the shoulder, right sides of work facing each other
At the neck edge hook up the 14sts at the top of the facing. The bulk of the WY makes the joining row difficult to knit. Remove it carefully, bringing the Ns out to HP first to avoid loosing sts.
K 1r T10
Cast off with the latch tool

SLEEVES (both alike)

With wrong side of garment facing, centre the shoulder seam at 0 at the armhole edge, the contrast markers at Ns80 on either side
Pick up evenly along armhole edge, bringing Ns out to HP to facilitate knitting the first row
Follow diagram for sleeve, working the fully fashioned shaping thus:
Using the 3×1 transfer tool, lift 3sts at once out of the first, second and third Ns from end, transfer to third, fourth and fifth Ns. Push the two empty Ns back to NWP
At RC 132, carr at R
K 1r T10
K 12rs T5
K 1r T10
K 12rs T5
K 1r T10
Finish on WY, release from machine

MAKING UP

Use one or two strands from the main yarn (Noil silk has three). Press with a warm, dry iron on the wrong side of work. At neck, fold collar band to inside and catch stitches on waste yarn to loose row, slip stitch ends of collar neatly. Sew pockets, leaving the 'pouch' free. Join side and sleeve seams. Fold hems and catch stitches on waste yarn to loose row.

At right front, unpick the buttonholes stitches very carefully. Using one strand of yarn, oversew each of the three sets of stitches separately, then oversew the hem buttonhole stitches together. Finally fold facing and slip stitch facing buttonhole to main buttonhole. Slip stitch the bottom of the facing to the bottom of the hem. Press again, on the wrong side. If necessary, lightly catch the facing to the front in one of two places. Do this carefully, or it will show on the front of the work. Sew feature button to correspond with the buttonhole. If you wish to insert shoulder pads, use the ones with velcro fastening for easy removal when washing. Medium weight iron-on Vilene will give a more structured look to the lapels. Iron onto the facing only.

GUERNSEY·STYLE·SWEATER

Guernsey yarn has a high degree of twist which, when knitted on a fairly tight tension, gives a hardwearing fabric which is as wind-proof and showerproof as any wool could expect to be. The machine quickly produces the wonderfully firm fabric achieved by patient hand knitting on fine gauge needles. Compromise has to be made for the details one expects on traditional hand-knitted garments, and in searching for a machine knitted equivalent without using a ribber, one creates a variation on the design rather than an imitation.

Knit your guernsey with a generous allowance for shirts, lightweight sweaters and any extra garments you are likely to wear underneath, and plenty of length to keep the lower back warm. It is meant to be an outdoor garment, worn over lightweight loose clothes. However its classic shape looks well in cotton and in woollen blends, though the sweater would no longer serve its original purpose as a wind and weather cheater.

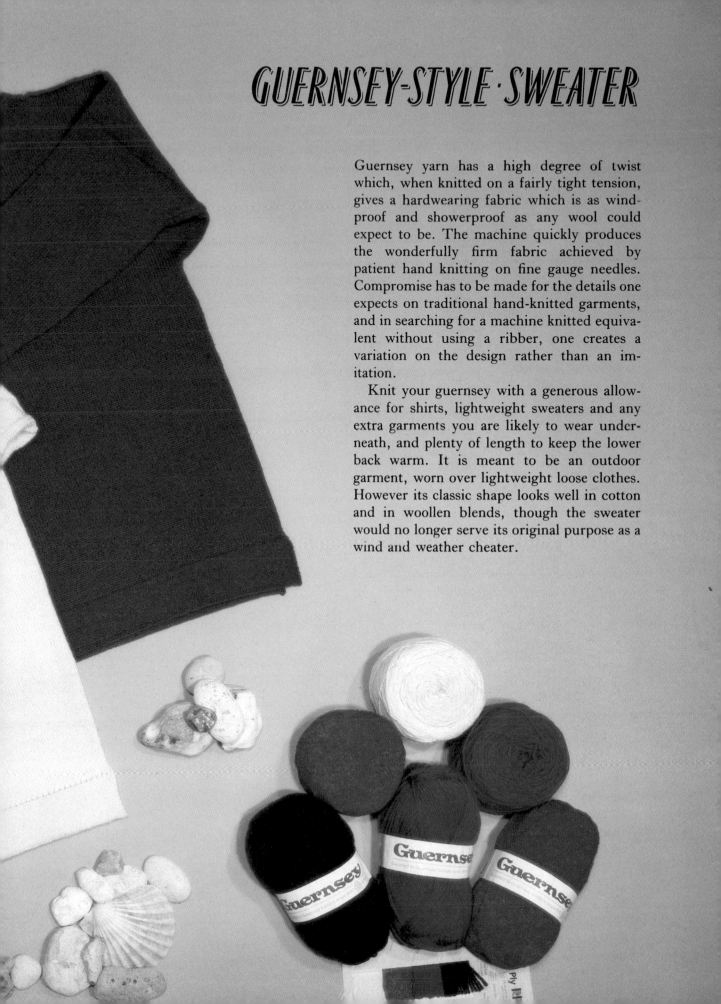

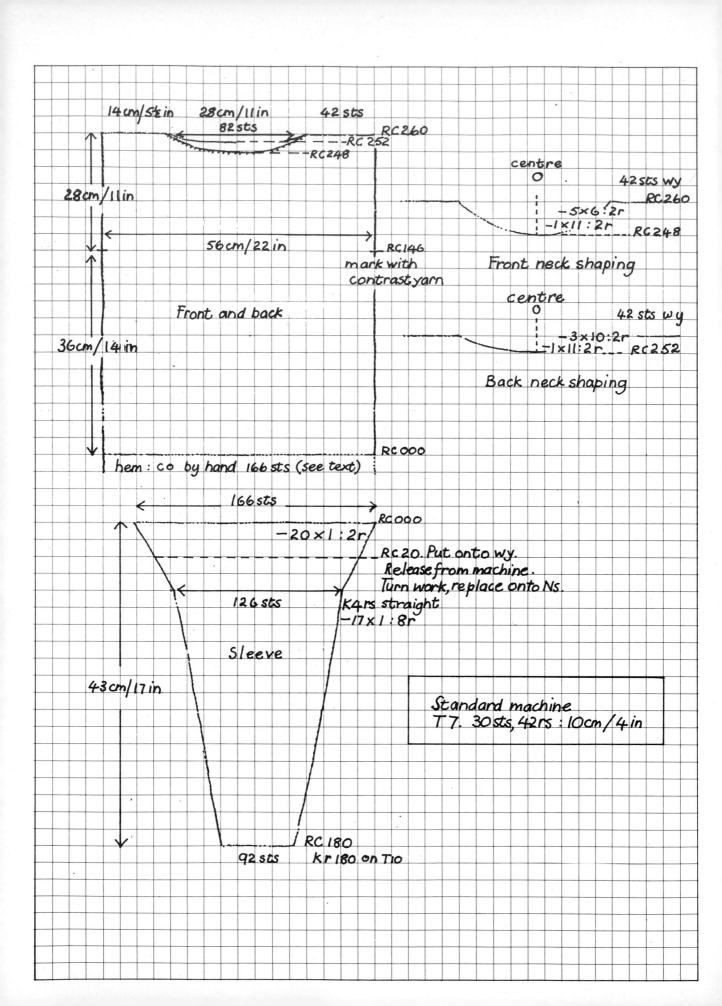

14 cm/5½ in   28 cm/11 in   42 sts
             82 sts
                                    RC 260
                              − − − − RC 252
                          − − − RC 248

28 cm/11 in

                                    centre
                                      O   42 sts wy
                                                 RC 260
                                            −5×6 :2r
                                        −1×11 :2r   RC 248

                          ← RC 146   Front neck shaping
          56 cm/22 in   mark with
                          contrast yarn
                                    centre
                                      O   42 sts wy
          Front and back
                                            −3×10:2r
                                        −1×11:2r   RC 252
36 cm/14 in
                                        Back neck shaping

                                    RC 000
        hem : co by hand 166 sts (see text)

             ← 166 sts →
                                    RC 000
                −20×1 : 2r
                                    Rc 20. Put onto wy.
                                    Release from machine.
                                    Turn work, replace onto Ns.
             ← 126 sts →   K4 rs straight
                                    −17×1 : 8r

             Sleeve

43 cm/17 in
                                    ┌─────────────────────────┐
                                    │ Standard machine   │
                                    │ T 7. 30 sts, 42 rs : 10 cm/4 in │
                                    └─────────────────────────┘

                          RC 180
             92 sts   kr 180 on T10

Yarn: Poppleton's 5 ply Guernsey, available in 100gm/3½oz balls which need to be wound and waxed for the machine. You will need between 800gm/28oz and 1,000gm/35oz to knit a sweater from 97cm/38in to 112cm/44in chest and up to 68cm/28in long

Machine: Standard

Tension: 17, giving 30sts and 42rs to a 10cm/4in square

Measurements: The diagram is calculated for a sweater measuring 112cm/44in chest, 66cm/26in long. Follow diagram for stitches, rows, and shaping

BOTTOM HEMS

These are hand cast on, and then reversed before turning up as follows:

Carr at R, bring every other N out to HP

Cast on by hand ('e' wrap) on the Ns at HP

Carr set for normal knitting

K 1r T7. Bring all Ns to WP

RC 000

Bring all Ns to HP on every row until you can hang weights

K 24rs T4

K 1r T10

K 26rs T4

K 1r T9

Carr at L. Remove MY, but do not break

K several rs WY, release hem from machine

With the right side of work facing, hook up the cast on edge onto Ns. The hand cast-on edge forms a chain, and can be put onto the Ns methodically with the double eyelet tool, the front strand on the right hand eyelet, the back strand on the left. If this is difficult, use the single eyelet tool, but always put the front strand up first, the back second, otherwise the decorative effect of the hem will be irregular

Turn up the hem, hooking up the sts on WY onto the corresponding Ns. The WY will be inside the knitting

FRONT AND BACK

RC 000. Carr at R

Follow diagrams, knitting first row

T10 (turn up row of hem)

Mark the beginning of armholes with a coloured marker

Shape the neck using holding position. See diagram for row numbers

When both sets of shoulder sts are on WY, and the sts for the neckband are at HP, knit the neckband as follows:

RC 000, T4

Dec 1st at both ends of rs2, 6, 10 and 14

K 2rs T3

K 1r T10

K 2rs T3

Inc 1st at both ends of rs20, 24, 28 and 32

Transfer stitches so that there are two on every other needle. Leave all Ns at WP

K 2rs MT. Break MY and leave neckline sts on WY

Joining the back to the front at the shoulders: Carr at R

With wrong side of the back facing, replace one set of shoulder sts onto machine. With right side of the front facing, replace the matching shoulder sts onto corresponding Ns

The shoulder seam will be on the outside of the sweater

K 1r T10, carr at L

Cast off with the single eyelet tool as follows:

Starting from L, lift half of the first st onto second N. The first st now stretches over the first and second Ns. Bring second N to HP. Take the yarn over the second N. Pull the second N back by the butt, pulling the yarn through the second st and half of the first

Now lift half of the new st onto the third N so that it stretches over the second and third N and cast off the third st together with half of the second

All the cast-off sts remain on the Ns and can be removed when casting off is finished

This makes a flexible shoulder seam, and a feature on the right side of the work

It is important to put the sts from the back shoulder onto the Ns first, otherwise you will have one seam lying differently from the other.

SLEEVES (both alike)

Carr at L

With the right side of the work facing, pick up along armhole edge. Centre the shoulder seam at O, the armhole markers at the correct N at either side

RC 000, MT7

K 20rs, decreasing both ends of alt rs 10 times

Remove MY from feeder, K several rs WY

Turn work so that wrong side of garment is facing. Replace sts onto Ns

Reset RC to 20

K 20rs, decreasing both ends of alt rs 10 times

RC 40

Continue to decrease according to diagram

K last row of main part of sleeve on T10

CUFFS

Transfer sts for a 2×1 mock rib, pushing back every third N to NWP

K 36rs T4

K 1r T10

K 36rs T4

K 1r T9

Bring all Ns to WP. Turn up the cuff, being careful to have a stitch on each empty needle

Cast off with the latch tool

2rs T10 should give the cuff sufficient flexibility to allow the sleeve to be pushed up easily, however if you prefer, cast off using the sinkers or by splitting the stitch (as at shoulder) for a more flexible finish.

MAKING UP

Damp press garment sections on the wrong side. Make sure the bottom hem is well pressed – the yarn is very springy – along the fold line. Back stitch side and underarm seams, mattress stitch the cuffs continuously from outside to inside forming a tube. Leave hem open front and back, slip stitching the edges together. Slip stitch neckband edges together at sides, fold neckband to right side, pin, and back stitch through last row. Remove waste yarn. Press seams.

TROUSERS

Use the charting device to ensure a perfect fit for trousers. For the finer check trousers fine nepp was used for the main yarn; a woollen-based yarn with brilliant flecks of colour giving it a random surface interest and a slight texture. The second yarn for the check pattern was a botany, 100% pure new wool. The trousers in the large check are Shetland, 100% pure new wool throughout. It is a good idea to have a flecked or mixed yarn for one of the colours in a two colour pattern as this is a lazy way to give the impression of more colour. Many Shetland yarns come in subtle and delightful mixtures and are very suitable, being warm to wear and easy to launder. Choose a darker or stronger toned yarn for the second colour, as this gives the pattern its dominance.

For a subtle look, use two yarns of the same colour but of totally different textures, for example black superwash wool for the main yarn with two ends of a black industrial bouclé run together with one end of black industrial lambswool for the second colour gives a shadow effect. Cream yarns combined in the same way also look rather special. Black wool for the main yarn with lurex for the pattern transforms the trousers for elegant evening wear.

A cotton and linen slubbed yarn, with a plain cotton yarn for the second colour, will give you trousers for cooler summer days, or warmer days in spring and autumn. Don't worry that these trousers will loose shape or produce 'knees' when you sit. One of the advantages of using a good quality woollen yarn is its springy nature – it will return to shape after washing and often even after resting overnight – and experience has shown that a cotton or cotton and linen mixture behaves in a similar accommodating fashion. However, it does produce a heavier fabric which 'drops' in wearing. This can be quite dramatic, the weight of the yarn can increase the length by as much as 5cm/2in, so this must be allowed for.

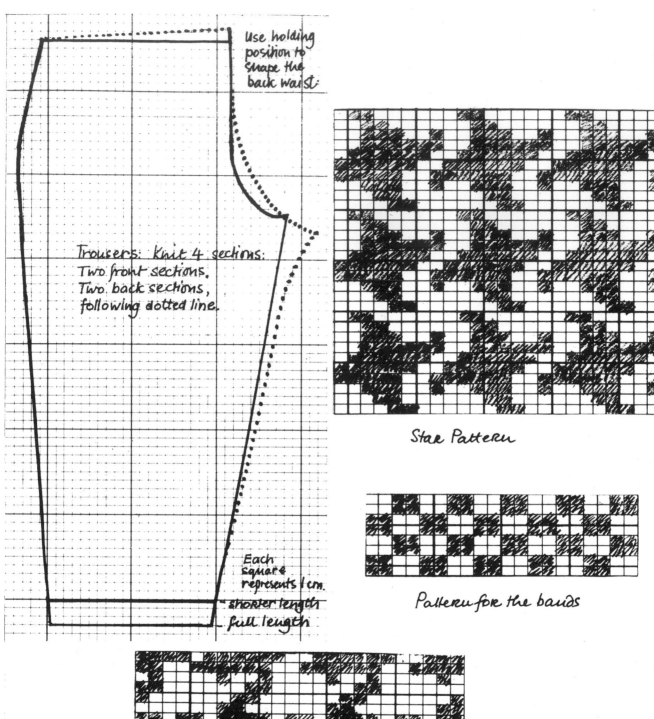

Use holding position to shape the back waist.

Trousers: Knit 4 sections.
Two front sections.
Two back sections,
following dotted line.

Each square represents 1 cm.

shorter length
full length

Star Pattern

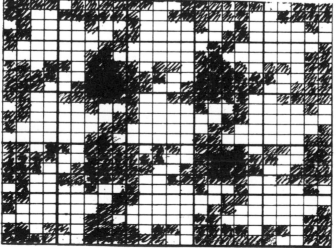

Pattern for the bands

Houndstooth Pattern

Yarn: Main yarn; Rowan Fine Nepp. 1 cone (350gm/12oz). Contrast: Rowan Botany, 1 cone (350gm/12oz). Or Jamieson Smith's 2 ply jumper weight (4 ply equivalent) 1 cone (455gm/16oz) each of main colour and contrast. The trousers use 230gm/8oz main colour, 170gm/6oz contrast

Also required: 2.5cm/1in elastic to measure waist plus 5cm/2in

Machine: Standard

Pattern cards: From the main set which comes with the machine

Measurements: The basic pattern given here is very flexible. Hip 86cm/34in to 102cm/40in, waist 61cm/24in to 86cm/34in. The length is also adjustable. The pattern is for a length of 80cm/31½in which gives a shortish trouser. If you want them longer add the required amount at the bottom of the pattern, allowing 4cm/1½in for the waistband and 5cm/2in for the ankleband. Width is easily added by extending the side seam. Remember 2cm/¾in added at each side will give an extra 8cm/3in altogether.

PATTERN NOTES

The trousers are made in four pieces, two fronts and two backs. Do this systematically to avoid getting into a muddle. On machines with transparent sheets you can knit a front, then a back, then turn the sheet around and feed it carefully into the device to knit the second front and back with the shapings reversed. Devices with paper sheets will need all four pieces drawn out separately.

Remember to follow the specific instructions for your charting device concerning tension square, stitch and row setting and drawing the pattern onto the pattern sheet.

Work a tension square, prepare and measure it. (If using Rowan yarn the tension square needs to be washed before measuring.) Draw the pattern onto your pattern sheet. Adjust stitch and row setting on the charting device. Check you don't confuse one with the other!

FRONTS AND BACKS

Cast on in waste yarn and work about 8rs ending with carr at L
Insert main Fair Isle pattern card, if used
Now with MY work 1 loose row, T8, setting the pattern if being used
Carr at R. Set tripper of charting device and knit, shaping as required, until the waist is reached
K 1r T8 in MY before knitting several rs of WY.
Release work from the machine
Work all four sections, shaping the backs at the waist using holding position and remembering to finish with one loose row when the shaping is finished before putting the stitches on waste yarn. This facilitates replacing stitches onto the machine for the waistband.

WAISTBAND

With wrong sides of backs facing, replace the waist stitches onto the needles thus:
Carr at L, MY in feeder 1
Centre backs at 0, miss sts1 and 2 and start by putting st3 on N1, st4 on N2 and so on
Then put st2 on N2 and st1 on N3, so there is one st on N1 and 2 on each of N2 and N3. This gives a seam allowance for making up
Check that all sts are picked up
Insert FI card for waistband pattern, if used
K 1r T9, setting pattern card
MY in feeder 1, contrast in feeder 2
RC 000

Release card
K 14rs T4, FI
Remove contrast yarn
Set carr for normal knitting, using MY:
K 1r T9
K 16rs T3
K 1r T9
Turn up a hem, picking up the corresponding sts from the first loose row
K 1r T10
Cast off with latch tool
If you are not patterning, the Fair Isle section for the waistband should be replaced by 16rs T3
Pick up and knit the front waistband in exactly the same way

ANKLE BANDS

Take care to organise the work correctly
Carr at L
With one front section and one back section, wrong sides facing you, sides to the centre, put up the stitches for the seam allowance as for the centre back
Now put 2sts onto N4 and 2sts onto every following third needle. This gathers the ankle slightly
K across all sts on T9, setting pattern
Work as for waistband, but knitting 18rs of FI and 20rs MY

MAKING UP

Press work. Join centre front and centre back seams in back stitch, matching the pattern. Join the waistbands at the sides, using mattress stitch, leaving the inside seam at the left open for the insertion of elastic. Join side seams, and finally the inside leg seams, using mattress stitch for the ankle bands. Secure all ends. Press seams on the inside and insert elastic to fit waist.

SIDEWAYS·KNITTED·FLARED·SKIRT

Knitted sideways, the full width of the needle-bed makes the length of this skirt. If you have already tried the practice pieces for holding position you'll understand more easily how the shaping is organised. Don't let 200 stitches intimidate you – it's surprising how quick and easy the skirt is to knit.

The cotton flecks in the fine nepp yarn used for the red skirt add colour and texture to the plain knit fabric. Alternatively you can put a simple Fair Isle pattern in the unshaped panels, making the skirt shape even more flattering. Two ends of bright courtelle run with one end of a fine bouclé would give a summer skirt with a lovely swing to it. There are really so many ways you can adapt this basic shape, which is one of the most successful methods of knitting a skirt.

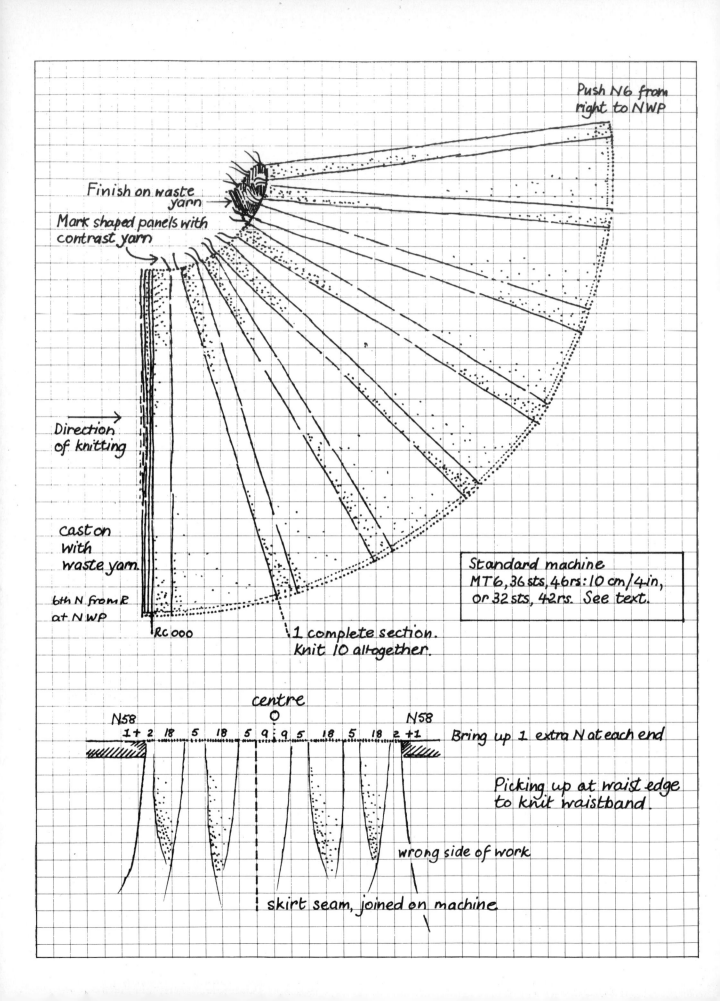

Push N6 from
right to NWP

Finish on waste
yarn

Mark shaped panels with
contrast yarn

Direction
of knitting

cast on
with
waste yarn.

6th N from R
at NWP

RC 000

Standard machine
MT6, 36 sts, 46 rs: 10 cm/4 in,
or 32 sts, 42 rs. See text.

1 complete section.
Knit 10 altogether.

centre
O

N58   N58

1 + 2 | 18 | 5 | 18 | 5 | 9 | 9 | 5 | 18 | 5 | 18 | 2 +1

Bring up 1 extra N at each end

Picking up at waist edge
to knit waistband.

wrong side of work

skirt seam, joined on machine

Yarn: Rowan Fine Nepp, 2 cones (500gm/17½oz) *or* Jamieson Smith's 2 ply jumper weight (4 ply equivalent) 1 cone (454gm/16oz) *or* strands of industrial yarns run together, eg 2 ends bright courtelle, 1 end bouclé

Also required: 2.5cm/1in elastic to measure waist plus 5cm/2in

Machine: Standard, 200 needles

Tension: MT6, giving 36sts, 46rs (for Rowan yarn, washed) to a 10cm/4in square; MT6, giving 32sts, 42rs (for Jamieson Smith's) to a 10cm/4in square

Measurements: Length without waistband 76cm/30in maximum, entire hem width 270cm/110in, maximum hip measurement 112cm/44in, waist adjustable to 92cm/36in

PATTERN NOTES

The style makes for very flexible fitting. In practice this is one garment where the measurement of the tension square is not crucial. Provided you use a yarn which is approximately 4 ply equivalent, it is really more important that it should handle sympathetically than be exact in tension. The hem can always be turned up a little more if the finished skirt seems too long.

Knitted sideways, you begin and end the skirt with waste yarn. The one seam is joined on the machine, stitches for the waistband are picked up in two sections, front and back. At the hemline one needle is left out of work, making it easy to turn the hem.

SKIRT

Bring 200Ns to WP. Push N95 at R back to NWP, where it will remain throughout the knitting
Cast on WY and K several rs, ending at L of machine
Join in MY
K 1r T8, carr at R
RC 000, MT6
* K 28rs, marking r1 and r28 with contrast yarn at L. This helps when picking up sts for the waistband
Carr at R, set to hold
Bring out 189sts to HP, starting from L of machine
K to L

Bring out N90 at R to HP
K to R
Replace 11Ns at R to UWP
K to L
Bring N80 at R to HP
K to R
Continue like this, shaping in groups of 10sts by pushing 11Ns back to UWP, K L, and bringing the last N knitted back to HP, thus wrapping the yarn, until all Ns are knitted back to WP and carr is at R
K 2rs
Carr still on hold
Bring out 9Ns at L to HP
K to L
Bring out tenth N at L to HP
K to R
Continue to knit, bringing groups of 10Ns to HP at L in this manner until all Ns from N100 at L to N90 at R are at HP and carr is at R *
You will find the carriage misses the row counter on the short rows at the right. This doesn't matter, since you can see where you are whilst you are shaping. However I always reset the row counter when knitting the 28rs straight.
Set carr to knit. Repeat from * to * nine more times to make ten panels in all. Mark the first and 28th row at L end of machine with a coloured marker to facilitate picking up the waistband
K 1r T8, carr at L
K several rs WY.
Release from machine

To join skirt at centre back: With right side of work facing, replace sts on WY onto the machine along one side. Fold up skirt and replace sts from the other side onto corresponding Ns. Wrong side of skirt is now facing
K 1r MY, T10
Cast off with the latch tool

WAISTBAND (in two sections)
Push 116Ns to WP
With the wrong side of the skirt facing, centre the first set of 28rs at waist edge at the centre of machine. The seam will be left of centre
Pick up 9sts to L and 9sts to R of 0 along the edge of this panel
Pick up 5sts along the edge of each shaped panel. You will have the

edges of 5 straight panels and 4 shaped panels on the machine
Now pick up 2sts from half of the shaped panel at each side. Bring up 1 extra N at each end (116sts altogether)
K 1r T8
K 19rs T3
K 1r T8
K 19rs T3
K 1r T8
Turn up a hem, picking up on the first loose row, to form the waistband
K 1r T10 and cast off with latch tool
Work the rest of the waistband to match

MAKING UP
If using Rowan yarn, wash the skirt before making up. Press the skirt, folding and pressing the little hem along the edge marked by the stitch at NWP. Slip stitch the hem invisibly to the skirt, or if you wish to use the sewing machine, choose a stitch suitable for jersey fabric using darker toned thread. This gives a very satisfactory finish and is almost invisible. Take care not to stretch the knitting or it will frill!

Slip stitch the waistband seams at the sides forming a casing, and leaving the inside seam at the left open for inserting elastic. Cut the length of elastic you require, plus 5cm/2in for overlap. Insert elastic into the waistband, overlap and sew the ends together.

VARIATIONS
The fullness of this design is very easy to regulate. If you want less width at the hips, shape at the left in two groups of 20 stitches instead of four groups of 10. If you want a shorter skirt, reduce the number of stitches at the bottom of the hem (the right of the machine) and adjust your grouping accordingly, starting your first group on a marked number for ease of working. If you are tempted to try a Fair Isle design, remember that the stitches in holding position will not knit back into pattern, so keep the Fair Isle for the straight sections.

It is sometimes difficult to find chunky yarns for the machine, and many knitters resort to buying expensive hand knitting yarns. Sale-time provided the hand-knit mohair for the contrast in this sweater, while the main yarn is a combination of two ends of nepp yarn with one end of industrial bouclé, making an inexpensive sweater. Since this is a beginners' design, and many beginners tend to produce uneven knitting when first using the intarsia carriage, using textured yarn helps to disguise any imperfections.

Mohair can be a pest when knitting, since its long fibres can catch on other yarns and on the sinkers, but you soon develop a habit of checking and correcting. The lovely texture of the mohair makes the extra effort worthwhile.

You can't expect to knit as quickly with the intarsia carriage as with the main carriage, but as compensation you have a tremendous amount of creative freedom. If the design on this page doesn't attract you, it's a very simple matter to use the chart for the shape only and incorporate your own design. It is equally easy to alter the yarns, using those of a similar thickness. Chunky cotton slub as the main yarn with novelty hand-knitting yarns for the contrast will transform this design into a summer sweater.

You can alter the shape too. This shape is 'cropped' – designed to come just to the waist. If you want to lengthen it, simply continue the contrast pattern down as far as you wish. The ratio graph paper used here makes alterations in size, pattern and design very simple. You can really see what you are doing.

Yarn: Main yarn: Rowan Fine Nepp, 1 cone (350gm/12oz) and fine industrial bouclé 150gm/5oz (2 ends of fine nepp and 1 end of bouclé are run together through one tension disc). Contrast: 25gm/1oz yellow mohair, 50gm/2oz each of cerise and turquoise mohair

Wind MY into 4 separate balls, yellow into 2, cerise and turquoise into 3 balls each

Machine: Chunky. If your machine has no built-in intarsia facility, you will need the separate intarsia carriage to work this design. An intarsia brake is an additional help, though not essential. It certainly controls the yarns.

Tension: T7, giving 20rs and 15sts to a 10cm/4in square. Adjust carriages to give the same tension

Measurements: Bust 112cm/44in, length 56cm/22in, sleeve length 38cm/15in

Whenever the intarsia pattern is not being knitted, the main carriage is used.

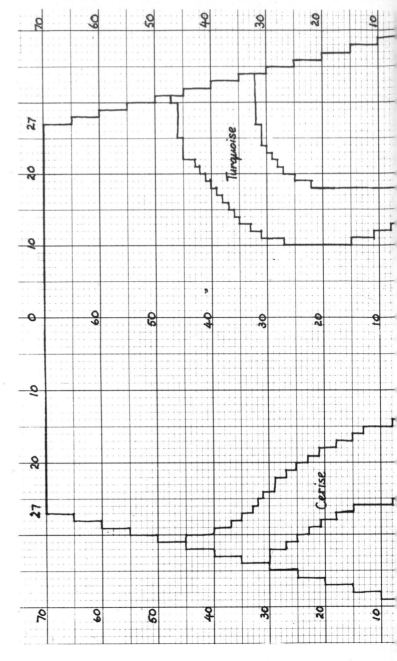

BOTTOM HEMS

Carr at R, cast on by hand 82sts

K 16rs T4, carr at R

Drop every other st 15rs down, and latch up to form rib (see Chapter 6)

When all sts have been latched up, set up the intarsia brake if used and change to the intarsia carriage, if used. Set up the Ns to UWP ready to lay in the colours for the first row (see the instructions with your machine or carriage)

Remember when laying in colours to start with the end or tail of the yarn nearest to the carriage

Always check that all stitches have knitted. The yarn MUST lie in the latches in order to knit, the stitches of the previous row being behind the latches.

FRONT

Follow the chart, laying in the colours, and marking the bottom of the armholes with a contrast marker

At RC 100, carr at R, begin neck shaping, using HP

The intarsia carriage will not K sts back from HP to WP. You will need to do this manually. When knitting the L side of the neck return the Ns to UWP ready for intarsia

Leave shoulder sts on WY. Bring out an extra needle at each end of the neckline sts

NECKBAND

Using main carriage K 1r T8

K 6rs T5

K 1r T8

K 6rs T5

Drop and latch up every other st to form a 13r rib

K 1r T8, break MY and leave on several rs WY

BACK

Work back, following chart, marking armholes as for front, working intarsia at shoulder

Leave shoulder and neckband sts on WY

SHOULDER SEAMS

Graft, using contrast yarn where necessary (see Appendix 4)

SLEEVES

Push up 80Ns to WP.

With shoulder seam at centre 0, markers at N40 either side, pick up evenly along armhole edge

120

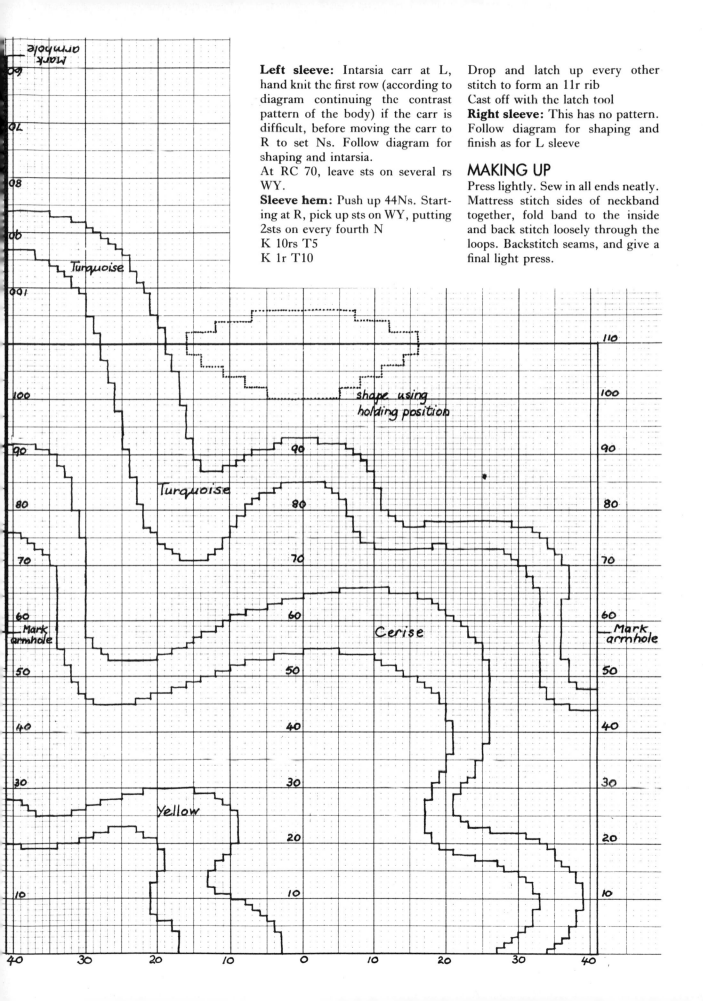

Left sleeve: Intarsia carr at L, hand knit the first row (according to diagram continuing the contrast pattern of the body) if the carr is difficult, before moving the carr to R to set Ns. Follow diagram for shaping and intarsia.

At RC 70, leave sts on several rs WY.

Sleeve hem: Push up 44Ns. Starting at R, pick up sts on WY, putting 2sts on every fourth N

K 10rs T5

K 1r T10

Drop and latch up every other stitch to form an 11r rib

Cast off with the latch tool

Right sleeve: This has no pattern. Follow diagram for shaping and finish as for L sleeve

MAKING UP

Press lightly. Sew in all ends neatly. Mattress stitch sides of neckband together, fold band to the inside and back stitch loosely through the loops. Backstitch seams, and give a final light press.

APPENDICES

1 Yarn Treatment and Garment Care

Synthetic fibres, nylon, terylene, dacron, orlon, acrilan and courtelle for example, though hardwearing and initially attractive, produce garments which tend to lose shape and pill. They are often blended with natural yarns – wool, cotton, silk or linen – to add strength. If your yarn has no care instructions but its content reveals the presence of synthetics, wash and press as for synthetic yarn. The hot iron suitable for cotton and linen will damage the synthetic element in a yarn which is a mixture of cotton, linen and acrylic. The rule for synthetics is to wash on a low temperature with a short spin, and to press when dry *without steam.* Press lightly on the wrong side with a cool iron. Bulky, 'mohair'-type synthetics are best left unpressed.

Wool and silk, and mixtures of these delicate yarns, should be washed by hand (unless marked machine washable) using a product specially developed for the care of delicate fibres. Spin out excess moisture, putting the garment in a pillowcase to protect from pulling and twisting. Ease gently into shape and dry flat away from heat. If you don't like putting luxury garments into the machine even to spin out excess moisture, then press and squeeze out as much water as you can by hand, but don't be tempted to twist or wring. Then lay a thick wad of newspaper on the floor, roll the garment loosely in an old towel and lay the roll onto the newspaper. Lean heavily on top to extract the moisture before leaving to dry flat. Press when dry with a warm iron for wool, cool for silk.

Cotton and linen will stand hotter and damper treatment. It is still preferable to wash by hand – since care and time has gone into the

WASHING	
Note: The washing symbols used by yarn companies vary. Some yarns labeled with just the tub and temperature are not always machine washable. Always take care when attempting to wash any yarn by machine that is not specifically called "machine washable."	
	DO NOT WASH BY HAND OR MACHINE
HAND	
	hand washable in lukewarm water only
40° C	hand washable in warm water at stated temperature
MACHINE	
6 40° C	machine washable in warm water at stated temperature, cool rinse and short spin; more delicate handling
7 40° C	machine washable in warm water at stated temperature, short spin
40° C	machine washable in warm water at stated temperature
Note: 40° C = approximately 100° F	
PRESSING	
	DO NOT PRESS
	press with a cool iron
	press with a warm iron
	press with a hot iron
DRY CLEANING	
	DO NOT DRY CLEAN
F	may be dry cleaned with fluorocarbon or petroleum based solvents only
P	may be dry cleaned with perchlorethylene or fluorocarbon or petroleum based solvents
A	may be dry cleaned with all solutions
Note: It may be necessary to ask your dry cleaner which solutions are used to clean your knitwear.	

Care symbols

making, the garment is worth the extra care when laundering. As both yarns are far less flexible than wool, the weight of water will pull them out of shape, so it is important to remove as much as you can and to dry garments flat. The iron for linen and cotton garments can be hot and set for steam if necessary. It is possible to iron directly onto the fabric, but preferable to protect it with a piece of cloth in case of accidents. Always press on the wrong side.

Finally, resist pressing ribbing. Welts can be gently pulled to shape when barely damp. If you must use an iron then hold it just above, but not touching the rib, perhaps with a piece of damp cloth on the knitting. Then gently pull the rib vertically. Never put an iron near a rib of synthetic yarn. Press means press – knitted garments should be pressed just as carefully as you pressed your tension square to avoid distortion. Ironing, the smoothing action you apply to pillow cases, cotton skirts and shirts, is not for knitted things.

2 Finishing

Knots are unsightly on a knitted garment, so weave in ends that have escaped machine finishing using a tapestry needle. These needles have blunt ends and don't split the yarn.

Most experts advocate blocking before making up. This entails pinning the garment

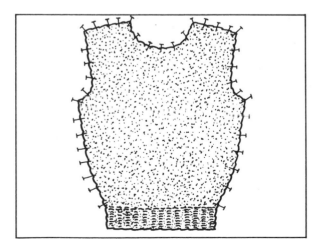

Garment blocking

pieces to size, wrong side up, onto a flat padded surface such as several thicknesses of old sheeting. Then dry, damp, or steam press, according to the yarn used, and allow the

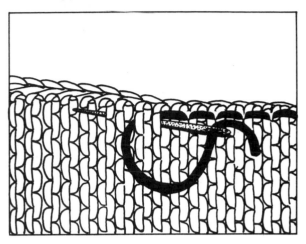

Back stitch

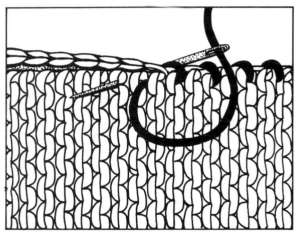

Oversewing

pieces to dry if necessary without distorting the shape. Follow the pressing advice given in Appendix 1.

Backstitch side and underarm seams, and slipstitch edges of pockets to garments. Oversew seams which need to lie flat, such as those in socks. Mattress stitch gives an invisible seam which is worth perfecting, especially when joining ribs. It is worked on the right side of the garment, so you are able to monitor your accuracy as you go along. Grafting is a method of joining two sections of knitting

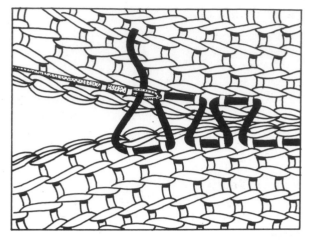

Mattress stitch

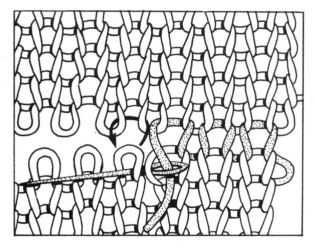

Grafting

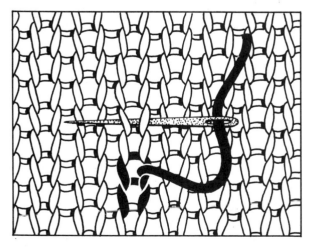

Swiss darning

which have been left on waste yarn – at the heel of a sock for example, occasionally at the shoulders, or the underarms seam of sideways-knitted garments if one wants an invisible join. A row of knitting is imitated using needle and yarn. To master the technique you have to get the 'stitch' size to match the knitting tension. Don't worry, it's easier than it sounds. Another imitative technique is Swiss darning which retraces the original stitch. It can be used to cover up small mistakes in patterning or to add extra colour where needed. Some knitters use this technique to embroider patterns on their work.

If you have used yarn in oil it has to be washed to reveal its true tension. I find it better to sew up these garments before washing, otherwise the resulting tangle of waste yarn and ends can be very daunting. Spin dry the washed garment or press the excess moisture out by rolling it in a towel. Shake it, gently pull into shape and dry on a flat surface, and leave it until barely damp before pressing. Never put sweaters on metal or wooden hangers.

Remember to wash, press and sew up with care; finishing can either perfect or ruin a garment.

3 Machine maintenance

Your machine is very robust. A minute of care before each knitting session will keep the carriage running smoothly and ensure that your machine lasts for years. First brush away fluff from the bed and beneath the carriage. Clean the bed with a cloth, then run the oil bottle lightly along the back rail, the needle butts, and the front rail. Occasionally dab a little oil on the moving parts beneath the carriage. If the brushes do not spin freely, unscrew them and remove any yarn and fibres causing this, and trim off any longer bristles. Cover your machine when it is not in use.

4 Further Reading

All machine manufacturers have stitch pattern and technique books available and some produce pattern books at regular intervals. If you write to them they will send you a complete list, but the most popular books should be stocked by your specialist shop.

When you begin to design for yourself you will find the strangest books can be inspiring. Books on foreign textiles and costumes, carpets and even geology can spark off original ideas for pattern and colour combinations. The fine and decorative arts section of your local library is a good place to start browsing.

Magazines will keep you up to date with what's going on in the machine knitting world. All these magazines are packed with advertisements for everything that could possibly interest the knitter and are a great source for addresses of mail order yarn suppliers.

Bond produce a bi-monthly magazine specifically for their machine and from time to time bring out pattern books in collaboration with various hand knitting wool companies.

Yarn Suppliers

The yarns used for the designs in this book are available internationally by mail order. Occasionally you may find that yarns have been deleted but spinners will always offer a suitable substitute.

Jamieson and Smith, 90 North Road, LERWICK, Shetland.
An extensive range of Shetland wool on the cone, bearing the woolmark. The best mail order company I know for prompt and efficient service to the customer!

Texere Yarns
College Mill, Barkerend Road, BRADFORD BD3 3AQ.
Glenora Craft Supplies, South Avondale Road, Dapto, New South Wales, Australia.
Gerald H. Whittaker Ltd/Inc, 12 Keefer Road, St Catherines, Ontario L2M7N9, Canada.
Gerald H. Whittaker Ltd/Inc, PO Box 35, 3255 Lockport Road, Niagara Falls, NY State 14305, USA.
An amazing selection of specialist yarns including silk, angora, mohair and many fancy yarns. Prices are sensible.

Celandine Ltd, 44 Kirkgate, OTLEY, West Yorkshire LS21 3HJ.
Exotic yarns including fox, racoon, mink and chinchilla. Not overpriced for the quality. They produce a very informative and helpful catalogue which includes wash care symbols for each yarn.

Rowan Yarns
Green Lane Mill, Washpit, Holmfirth, HUDDERSFIELD, West Yorkshire HD7 1RW.
Rowan Yarns, Rowan/Estelle Designs, 38 Continental Place, Scarborough, Ontario M1R2T4, Canada.
Westminster Trading Corp, 5 Northern Blvd, Amherst, NH 03031, USA.
A great variety of yarns in extensive and delightful colour ranges, and not overpriced, considering the quality. Woolmark where applicable. Their fine nepp yarn is particularly lovely.

Atkinson Mail Order Yarns
Canal Street, South Wigston, LEICESTER LE8 2PP.
Cardinits, 92 Cardinal Drive, Hamilton, Ontario L9A4H7, Canada.
Heart of Texas, Star Route, Box 1830, Burnet, Texas 87611, USA.
The catalogue is well produced and very informative, giving a range of interesting yarn mixtures each with the wash care symbol.

Richard Poppleton and Sons
Albert Mills, Horbury, WAKEFIELD, West Yorkshire WF4 5NJ.
Wendy Wools (NZ) Ltd, PO Box 29107, Greenwoods Corner, Auckland 3, New Zealand. (Australia and New Zealand).
White Buffalo Mills Ltd, 545 Assiniboine Avenue, Brandon, Manitoba R7A0G3, Canada. (USA and Canada).
The best Guernsey yarn there is. Unfortunately it is not on cone but the quality is worth the extra effort spent waxing and winding.

ACKNOWLEDGEMENTS

I would like to thank the knitting machine manufacturers for photographs and information. Particular thanks go to Pfaff and Brother for the generous loan of machines and accessories, to Norman Foster and Cornelia Gesell of Pfaff and to The Machine Knitting Division of Brother for their enthusiastic help. David Robinson of Alternative Sitting, Abingdon, is concerned that people should sit comfortably at their machines and loaned a specially-designed stool to prove it. The ready co-operation of Atkinsons, Celandine, Poppleton, Rowan Yarns, Texere and Jamieson and Smith, has made knitting for this book with their lovely yarns a pleasure. In providing True Knit and True Sew papers for design work, H. W. Peel and Co have been invaluable. Closer to home, Geoff and Pauline Bishop of Just Knitting in Tunbridge Wells are proof of how wise it is to support your local machine knitting shop. Thanks also to Tricot Products of Somerton for supplying me with their intarsia brake.

Anthony Caffyn very kindly turned his photographic skills from much-loved landscape subjects to 'interior with machines' for the benefit of this book. Thanks too to my daughter Louise who may sometimes have regretted that she ever learned to type while working on the manuscript, but who has benefitted by learning to knit whilst doing so. To all my students who inspire me as I hope I encourage them, and to Bobby Meyer who started it all, thanks!

INDEX

Illustrations are shown in *italic* type